All I Hold Dear

Poems on God, Family, and Country

DR. PAUL VEACH

ISBN 978-1-68197-874-1 (Paperback)
ISBN 978-1-68197-876-5 (Hard Cover)
ISBN 978-1-68197-875-8 (Digital)

Front cover photo credit: Vonda Murdock
Back cover photo credit: Rachel Veach

Christian Faith Publishing, Inc.
296 Chestnut Street
Meadville, PA 16335
www.christianfaithpublishing.com

Printed in the United States of America

ACKNOWLEDGMENT

I wish to acknowledge the efforts of my wife, Rachel, who, for nearly forty years, has served as my secretary, confidante, sounding board, editor, bookkeeper, typist, and supplier of foods and snacks. This book would not have been possible without her patient help.

AUTHOR'S NOTE

From where does a poem come? I suspect that's a question with many answers; each person who writes poetry (I blanch at the title "poet"), I'm sure, has a methodology that prompts the creative process in them. I am a harvester of phrases.

In my younger years, I jotted down phrases I saw on posters, greeting cards, and in gift shops. These phrases were integrated, in whole or in part, into my poems or were used as a catalyst to initiate a poem. As I matured (some deny that process has even begun) and my relationship with the Lord grew, many of the phrases I collected were heard during sermons, while reading the scripture, or during my devotional time.

Og Mandino, in his book *The Greatest Miracle in the World*, introduced a character, Simon Potter, who was what he called a "Rag Picker." This was someone who picked up rags discarded by others, cleaned them, and made them useful again. Simon's real purpose, however, was to pick up people relegated to the rag piles of life, and through encouragement, return their lives to usefulness once again. This book spoke to my heart when I first read it in 1978 as a young man of nineteen. I determined at that young age that *this* was the person I wanted to become in my life. A rag picker. God put within my heart a desire to offer encouragement and hope to the discouraged and defeated and that drove my decision to become a medical doctor. Now at the age of fifty seven, whether my life has in any part been a source of encouragement to my fellow man will be for others to decide.

At that time and to this end, I wrote a vision statement for myself, a sort of "waymark" (Jeremiah 31:21) in my life that I still use and have included at the end of these remarks.

In many respects, my poetry is an extension of my rag-picking efforts. Since I gave my heart to Jesus Christ at age seventeen, I have endeavored to encourage and uplift others who may live in despair and discouragement. Similarly, my poems were often written in melancholy mood—not depression, mind you! I find that in melancholy times I am more introspective; when I am alone (and this is hard for a sanguine personality), I am able to converse openly with God and the poems ultimately flow in recollection of those times of close fellowship.

I also recognize that one of the more painful experiences in life is to have to read poems written by amateurs like me… so if your spouse is forcing you to read one of my poems, or worse yet, it is some sort of a bizarre job prerequisite (you should seriously seek other employment), I am profoundly sorry. But not repentant.

My waymark:

"I am first a servant, living my life in the service of others. Even though this opens my life up to possible abuse by others, I will endeavor to be a servant nonetheless. I will live a life of integrity, seeking to honor God, my family, and my country. I will live a passionate life and seek to encourage others. Through a close relationship with God, I will put aside fear and anger and instead live a life filled with gratitude and humor. I am a Rag Picker."

(Written in its original form in 1978 and carried in my wallet since.)

FOREWORD

Poetry, like the artist's sketch or canvas work, is often left to personal interpretation. I have marveled at times by what I perceived of an artist's interpretation versus my own. Dr. Veach has done us a great service in these "Poems on God, Family and Country." He gives us the backstory. This adds a touch of relief and understanding to sometimes a complicated process of interpretation.

How well I remember the first time I met Paul and his wife Rachel. Here was a busy medical doctor who took his vacation time to come to Canada and help plant a church. Not only does he care for the general physical health of people, but also their souls.

Poetry ministers to the soul. Knowing what events or thoughts brought the inspiration, puts the readers in the author's shoes and they join in the emotion of the time.

You will be blessed as you read, and I believe your appreciation for poetry will be enhanced. I know mine has been.

It gives me great pleasure to recommend this book and I am honored to call Dr. Paul Veach my friend.

Michael Sullivant
Senior Pastor
Pembina Valley Baptist Church
Winkler, Manitoba, Canada
2016

Contents

II.   Poems on Family and Home

III.   Poems on Country and the Dream

IV. Tributes

I

◆

Poems on God

THE SACRIFICE

I read one time that God showed His love when He spread out His arms... and died. I turned that phrase over and over in my mind and finally put pen to paper in the poem "The Sacrifice."

Some have recommended a change in the third line, "The labor's wage..." implying that I meant to say "laborer's wage," but it is not so. My thought was that all work, or labor, has a price and this is the wage of that labor. In a veiled reference, additionally, I wanted to hint at the idea that there was little sacrifice for the workman who made the cross but the wage of his work in the flesh was actually death (Romans 3:23), and that is a different matter altogether.

(August 28, 1985)

The Sacrifice

The wood was from an aged tree,
    The nails, a penny's price
The labor's wage was paid in full,
    So small their sacrifice.

Judgment made for man's favor,
    Pilot's power did entice;
He washed his hands in water pure,
    So small his sacrifice.

The path was short for strengthened legs,
    The people thronged the way;
The cross, light, for the soldier's arms,
    No sacrifice he'd pay.

No sacrifice, there was no price,
    For none of these to pay,
But Jesus left His Father's home,
    To come to earth one day.

Trading heaven's splendor,
    For death upon the tree,
Knowing He'd endure the pain,
    If only but for me.

What sacrifice, how great the price,
    I see within His eyes;
The King of Glory bows His head,
    ... spreads His arms and dies.

BLESSED REASSURANCE

In the fall of 1985, I made the decision to leave the Air Force and go to medical school. In the fall of 1987, as my separation date of March 18, 1988, drew closer, I became increasingly anxious. Even though I was confident this was the plan of God for my life, I think I doubted the provision of God. I found myself pacing the floor at night, attacked by doubt. I was not so concerned for myself but was concerned I was leading my family into unnecessary hardship.

As I opened the Word of God in the quiet of night, I found myself reading in Isaiah 32:17, 18 about the assurance of God when a man lives in righteousness: "And the work of righteousness shall be peace; and the effect of righteousness quietness and assurance forever. And my people shall dwell in a peaceable habitation, and in sure dwellings, and in quiet resting places."

I had my reassurance…

(October 15, 1987)

Blessed Reassurance

When the night is as black as it's ever been
    And the sound of the dark hushes still,
In the abyss of the night, reassure me, Lord,
    That I stand in the midst of Thy will.

When assassins of doubt as an army assail
    And the path that I walk grows obscure;
Though encompassed about by this enemy, doubt
    Oh, Lord, Thou my vision restore.

Reassure me, Lord, reassure me, Lord,
    That I stand in the midst of Thy will,
Let me see Thy face, with Your love, close embrace,
    Oh, Lord, reassure me still.

When Satan attacks with his demons of might
    And his forces about me encamp
May I look to the stronghold with eyes of faith
    With Thy Word held aloft as a lamp.

When friends disappoint and my way lonely grows
    And the bands of the wicked grow taut
At midnight I'll rise to give thanks unto Thee
    Giving praise for the peace Thy blood bought.

When I stand at the place where two paths diverge
    And I question what lieth ahead
May I face the future with strengthened faith,
    In trust, to walk where You've led.

Reassure me, Lord, reassure me, Lord,
    That I stand in the midst of Thy will
Let me see Thy face, with your love, close embrace
    Oh, Lord, reassure me still.

THE MASTER'S EYES

During the months leading up to start medical school, my wife and I (and our daughter) moved to Columbia, South Carolina. While there, we attended Grace Baptist Church in West Columbia that was pastored by Clayton Shumpert at the time.

He preached a sermon on Zacchaeus in the tree straining to see Jesus. He used the four phrases "He sees you," "He knows you," "He wants you," and "He loves you" as an outline of his sermon. That struck a responsive chord with me, and I meditated on that sermon for several weeks. On March 13, 1990, God gave me this poem using the four points of Pastor Shumpert's sermon.

I had contemplated the joy in the heart of a person, so rejected all their life because of a physical ailment or condition, then coming to the realization that they are loved, truly *loved*, in the eyes of God.

(March 13, 1990)

The Master's Eyes

"He sees me!" came the whispered cry
    Of Zacchaeus in the tree.
"But I have been an evil man,
    How can He look on me?"

He must see the depth of sin
    Into which I've been so mired—
And like a beast, I felt so trapped
    I struggled then grew tired.

"He knows me!" Came the anxious voice,
    While he sat upon the limb.
But I have buried thoughts so deep
    Are they revealed to Him?

Surely He must know the type
    Of man I've been, and worse,
The type of thoughts I've harbored deep,
    Am I a man accursed?

"He wants me!" cried the joyful heart.
    He can't! None ever could!
How can He want a man so scorned?
    Yet beneath the tree He stood.

How can it be He calls my name
    In spite of all I've done?
Could it be that below me stands
    My Master, God's own Son?

"He loves me!" wept the broken heart.
    He sees through my disguise,
A sinner, vile to others, yet
    Loved in the Master's eyes!

INSCRIBED NAILS

While listening to a sermon in Columbia, SC, I heard my pastor use the phrase, "Inscribed on the nail that was pounded into our Savior's hands and feet was God's love."

That thought echoed in my mind all week as I meditated on the truth of that statement. I considered how Christ not only died on the cross but also purposefully loosed the load of sin from my back and willfully took on Himself the penalty I deserved. All this for the cause of His love.

I wrote this poem from that perspective—that I was in prison and being required to pay for my own sins. His mercy and love stepped out, however, and He took on Himself my death sentence. Truly, at Calvary, Psalm 85:10 was fulfilled: "Mercy and truth are met together; righteousness and peace have kissed each other."

(May 23, 1992)

Inscribed Nails

A captive in prison, a price on my head
    For my crimes still I had yet to pay;
The turmoil around me had settled within,
    In my life, no peace but dismay.

I stood at the trial, my body in chains
    Without hope, I was holding my breath
I lowered my head as the sentence was read,
    For my crimes had demanded death.

The list of my sins were now strapped to my back
    And I fell 'neath the weight of the load;
I pleaded for mercy, but the voice of the crowd
    Was harsh as I trudged Calvary's road.

But the roar hushed to silence when forth from their midst
    Strode a man clad in robes pearly white;
His face so tender and His eyes full of love
    Pitied my soul and pierced through my night.

He spoke with such peace; what compassion He had.
    I trembled as tears bathed His face;
And the words He then spake caused my hard heart to break,
    "Loose his load for I'm taking his place."

I stood then alone at the foot of His cross
    He who loved me in spite of the thorns,
Knowing His nails held the list of my sins
    Each inscribed on the spike as a scorn.

Through His pain, so intense, His eyes sought mine own
    As if showing God's purpose above
And I wept when I saw, as He opened His hand,
    Inscribed simply on the nail was "God's Love."

INSUFFICIENT

I wrote this poem the day after I wrote "Inscribed Nails" mostly because I had spent over a week contemplating my Pastor's sermon (see explanation on "Inscribed Nails") and felt like the former poem did not complete my thoughts on the subject.

I also wanted to explore Christ's sacrifice and great love—juxtaposed with my shamefulness. Shameful that when I am called to stand for Christ, too often I cowardly sink back into the shadows... shameful that, too often, when I think I am strong, it is only my self-righteousness on display... and shameful that too frequently pride effaces humility.

The title, to me, says it all. *Insufficient.* When we stand in our own strength, we are all insufficient. God calls us to more. He calls us to walk in humility, submitted to the Holy Spirit moment by moment. In this way, anger, frustration, aggravation, worry, fear, and irritation—all fall in the face of submission.

(May 24, 1992)

Insufficient

The stripes I did not feel
    Nor the crown upon His brow
While the battle raged in full
    ... I stayed behind somehow.

As they spat upon His face
    He withheld His Father's might
While the battle raged in full
    ... I escaped into the night.

The battle raged around me
    And I—a soldier weak
While the Savior stood alone
    His strength I did not seek.

I thought my strength sufficient
    To face the fight alone
But I see my arm is weary
    If Your strength I'd only known.

Fit me, a soldier, strengthened
    With power to fight anew,
Not in my pride, this battle,
    The flesh within subdue.

Make me a warrior ready
    To face the foes ahead,
Fit me with humbled spirit
    To walk where Thou hast led.

ONCE MORE ROUND

Carl Boonstra, the great missions speaker, was a guest speaker at a church I was attending on March 28, 1996, and he used as his text Joel 3:11–14. He called attention especially to verse 13, "Put ye in the sickle, for the harvest is ripe: come, get you down; for the press is full, the fats overflow; for their wickedness is great." The mental image that came to my mind was a farmer feverishly working to get the harvest in before the gathering storms broke upon the field.

(March 28, 1996)

Once More Round

"Once more round, my children, now hasten to labor,
　　For the harvest in peril now lies,
Encircle the field, once more round, oh, children
　　For warning signs darken the skies!"

Storm clouds, once distant, on fields now approaching,
　　How long ere the harvest be lost?
"Once more round!" the Master calleth to workers.
　　"To combines, tarry not for the cost."

Put ye in the sickle for the harvest is ripe,
　　The press and the fats overflow,
The harvest, soon bent, from hailstorms of judgment,
　　Still the Master stands pleading, "Will you go?"

"Will you go? Will you go?" the Master stands crying.
　　"To the field more workers I need!"
The harvest, near past, soon the trumpet will blast,
　　"Once more round..." the Master yet pleads.

Photo Credit: Rachel Veach

ONE DAY

On January 24, 2007, while working as the physician in an emergency room, I suffered a stroke that took away my ability to use the right side of my body. The following days and weeks were a blur with hyperbaric oxygen therapy (not an accepted practice in the US but used with good success in Europe) and physical therapy. God was very merciful as I eventually regained 80 percent function in my arm and leg.

In spite of the physical struggle, I was at peace spiritually. I knew that if God was calling me home, I was ready, although saddened for the heartache I might leave behind. Each of us will stand before God, one day, either by death or by rapture. I am thankful that the White Throne Judgment is not in my future but the prospect of standing before God, face-to-face, giving account of my life is still a sobering thought.

What might He say?

(March 28, 1996)

One Day

A faithful servant I would be
    Inspired by God's love for me.
From sin and bondage set me free
    His precious blood my only plea.

And soon one day I'll see His face
    My life displayed, I'll plead my case
And hear, "You're faithful, take thy place"
    Or hear "Your works, your pride efface."

Death or rapture, either way
    One will strike this lump of clay
And from gray skies to Heaven's day
    This wearied body down I'll lay.

From earthly blight to Heaven's bright
    From mortal plight to Holy light
From darkened glass to perfect sight
    O, may my life bring God delight.

That in this life I'd faithful be
    And help lost souls redemption see
In my flesh my pride I'd flee
    And Holy like my Savior be.

So help me, God, this I pray,
    Give what I need not what I say;
Help me serve, submit, obey
    And walk in truth and never stray.

A PLAY IN FOUR ACTS

By far, this was the hardest poem I have ever written. As a family in February 2010, we faced a spiritual struggle. This led us to join hands with a Pastor God had called to the local area and assist him in establishing a true Bible-based church. His ministry was geared to teaching people to develop a real relationship with God and helping them to develop spiritual maturity. His ministry was to hurting people, and we were hurting.

Through the early months of this ministry, the sermons were difficult to endure because of the conviction of the Holy Spirit. God allowed me to evaluate my life as a whole, and this poem was my honest assessment of that process.

Dividing my life into four segments, I evaluated each in light of God's Word. I examined my life as a son, a husband, a doctor, and a father. As a son, I recall the anger behind my joking facade and the pain it doubtlessly caused my parents. As a husband, I felt I had done well, but frankly, it was not without a lot of time reading the Word of God and, I confess, hundreds of marriage books! It took a while to get to the doctor phase but what a joy this aspect of my life has been. In honest evaluation of my role as a father, however, I realized I had made so many mistakes in ignorance. Sometimes the anger from my childhood resurfaced, and I wounded others with angry words. I had lost the heart of several of my children through anger and angry words. I praise God that, in the years since the start of the new church, God has allowed the restoration of those relationships. This poem was written at a time when those relationships were still fractured and the move to the new church was still fresh.

(April 26, 2010)

A Play in Four Acts

The last act of the play is now o'er,
    And they softly dim the light.
The curtain above lowers down on the scene,
    As the actor exits stage right.

With lowered eyes, he walks to the wings,
    Where loved ones offer words, kind.
Praise is given for the part he played,
    Yet doubts remain in his mind.

"Act 1, when I played the part of the 'son,'
    Within me I sensed a rage;
I regret I brought hurt to those I loved
    With whom I had shared the stage.

"Act 2, this scene, a 'husband' was I,
    (at first, my lines were all wrong),
    But devoted, I poured my heart in this part,
This scene I feel finished quite strong.

"The role of 'doctor' I played in act 3,
    Though slowly unfolded this part,
A pleasure it was to have acted this scene,
    And comfort the aching heart.

"Alas, I come to the act of great shame,"
    (I speak of the final act, four)
"My lines were twisted and spoken in haste."
    (As he lowered his eyes to the floor.)

"Act 4 was the scene where 'father' I played,
    To five actors who on stage viewed my flaws,
Hasty words betrayed the love in my heart,
    I recoil at the hurt that I caused."

So the curtain now falls on this play in four acts,
    Will the audience, I wonder, be kind?
In review of the life portrayed in this play,
    My words, were they gentle they'd find?

The Author! The Author! And oh, what of Him?
    The One whose praise I most sought,
Was He pleased with the play He witnessed tonight?
    And honor to Him have I brought?

Curtain down, off stage walks the actor,
    Deaf to applause he had won,
Straining to hear the Author's words he had sought
    Would he hear the soft-spoken "Well done?"

FISH FOR LESS

I really loved the phrasing in this poem. The idea came from a phrase mentioned in passing in a sermon my pastor preached: "God wants you to be selfless not selfish."

I started this poem with the last line and worked my way backward. This thought summarizes the struggle in a Christian's life: serving God or pleasing self. One way provides instant pleasure but reaps eternal loss—the other brings self-sacrifice but eternal gain. I recall a short poem in my youth: "Two choices on the shelf, pleasing God or pleasing self."

And that is the Christian struggle.

(May 24, 2010)

Fish for Less

I have lost many a thing,
    Some I'll never find
But the greatest thing that I have lost?
    This great fish of mine.

This fish was closer than a friend,
    A constant companion, he
But lose him I must, if ever I would,
    Become what God meant me to be.

So what would I gain if I lose my fish?
    And, Lord, on my heart impress?"
"I'll exchange your fish for something more
    What I will give you is less."

Less to gain is the heart of God,
    Though contrary I thought, I confess
He has given me less in losing my fish,
    In exchanging selfish for selfless.

A DOOR OF HOPE

In August 2010, Rachel and I recorded our fourth vocal CD. We titled it "A Door of Hope," and in October 2010, I submitted this poem for inclusion on the inside fold-over. The CD also had imprinted a picture of the door to the empty tomb, the *real* "door of hope." That empty tomb speaks truth to the claims of Jesus Christ, and apart from a real relationship with Christ, there is no hope.

This poem was written as a song, and we had intended to record it on this CD, but were not able to do so. Notice within the poem there are "action steps" required on the part of the reader. Many people say they want a close relationship with God but are unwilling to do the "action steps" required. They may *want* to live holy lives but are unwilling to choose to control their thoughts; they may want to have a close relationship instead of a mechanical one but are unwilling to spend quality time with Him daily in His Word. The true essence of hope in a person's life is seen in the fifth stanza, "I found peace when I longed to know you." This hope is in a relationship with Christ through the Word of God.

It is so sad that we live in a microwave society. Unfortunately, many Christians have adopted this microwave pattern in their daily devotions. They read a one-minute devotional, read a few verses, and feel they have "met with God." I'm not saying this is not possible, just that in my understanding of the Word of God, a relationship is built on time spent together. I wonder how long we would be married to our spouse if we only spent the amount of time with them that we offer God? Longing to know Christ takes a commitment of our time.

(October 1, 2010)

Photo Credit: Rachel Veach

A Door of Hope

Caught in a whirlwind of defeat and despair,
 In turmoil, no peace could I see,
Yearning to find a safe haven of rest,
 Crying aloud, "Is hope there for me?"

Then a door of hope was opened for me,
 "Enter and rest you will find,"
A fountain of mercy, His grace flowing free,
 Contentment and peace for your mind.

Traveling alone or so it had seemed,
 Failing in all eyes that I knew;
Wanting to change, but not knowing the way,
 Hope gone, with no help in view.

Then a door of Hope was opened to me,
 "Enter, forgiven of sin,"
Step o'er the threshold and lay burdens down,
 For here are lives changed from within.

Yes, the door of Hope was opened for me
 I entered and peace given new,
The source of all Mercy longed to know me;
 I found peace when I longed to know You.

A door of Hope was opened for me,
 "Enter and rest you will find,"
A fountain of mercy, His grace flowing free,
 Contentment and peace for your mind…

Contentment and peace for your mind.

SERVANT LEADERSHIP

In June 2011, I was asked to give a talk to a large group of ER physicians. Since many of the doctors were in positions of leadership, I chose as my topic "Servant Leadership." In preparation for this talk, I read a great number of books, speeches, and articles in an attempt to distill the concept into the base essentials.

I started my list with twenty essentials, cut it to ten, and then pared the list to five. I could not see how the list could be shorter. In my devotions one morning, however, I read Psalm 51, David's great psalm of repentance. As I pondered that psalm, I considered how David, the greatest king of Israel, realized how his sin had harmed his nation and repented before God, yearning His fellowship once again.

With this as my backdrop, I wrote this poem as I came to the understanding that true servant leadership, like in David's life, comes first with a bowing in repentance before God and a yearning for His fellowship.

(June 13, 2011)

Servant Leadership

How can I teach, if I myself do not obey?
    If time within Thy Word, I do not spend today?
If before Thy holy throne, I do not prostrate lay?
    Why should one even hear me, or heed the words I say?

My words have only healing when mirrored from Thy Word,
    Others only hear me when from Thy book I've heard,
For help is not within me, my wisdom not assured,
    My words are tinkling symbols, if from Thy Book I'm lured.

A servant's heart I ask of Thee, that I might reach another,
    Submitted to Thy plan for me, that I might help my brother,
To know Thee, Lord, is wisdom's truth; this is treasure, true:
    That servant leadership begins... in my fellowship with you.

EARS TO HEAR

In His condemnation of the Laodicean Church, God described them as blind, wretched, poor, and desperately needy. Yet the "self-image" of the apostate church is the exact opposite of God's description. This is the sadness of the hour in most churches. They are content to hold a high opinion of themselves, unaware of how far they have strayed from honoring God. We live in an age where positive self-image rules, even in churches!

As I was reading Revelation 3:14–22, I considered those things. I asked God if those same qualities were in me. How would I know if I was blind, except the Holy Spirit reveals it to me? Or wretched, while thinking I have need of nothing? I suspect all of us have blind spots in our lives—areas we don't see needing to change yet God *knows* we need to change them. If we never ask God about our blind spots, our spiritual growth is hindered.

This poem was written in response to the passage in Revelation and reflected the convicting of the Holy Spirit in my life.

(June 13, 2011)

Ears to Hear

Wretched and poor, blind and in need,
    I bow at the throne of Thy grace,
Thinking that all that I thought that I had,
    Would suffice to win in this race.

Insufficient, however, the works of my hands,
    The deeds and goods that I've won,
All these are loss, in the fire consumed,
    When I stand at the throne of Thy Son.

Gold tried in fire, white raiment I need,
    And eye salve that I mayest see,
An ear tuned to hearing truth that is taught,
    Repentance and bowing the knee.

As I open Thy Word, Lord, open my heart,
    And show where change must be made,
Submitting myself to the Lamp of Thy Word,
    Obeying all You have said.

Grant me, oh, God, ears that hear truth,
    And eyes that are longing to see,
Humble and broken, giving heed to Thy Word,
    Surrendered in fullness to Thee.

HEAR AM I

No, I didn't misspell the title of this poem. Before being willing to hear the Holy Spirit, Isaiah in chapter six had a live coal placed to his lips. What is the significance of this? Revelation 4:5 describes that there are seven lamps of fire burning before the throne, which are the seven Spirits of God. Isaiah 11:2 describes the seven Spirits, and in Isaiah 6, the Seraphim picked a hot coal from off the altar before God's throne. Isaiah recognized his uncleanness and from before the throne, the coal, representing the holiness of God, made him prepared to speak with God. With his sins removed from him by the holiness of God, Isaiah was now in a position to *hear* God.

As I read that passage on September 8, 2001, it occurred to me that I had to be able to "hear" God before I could say "*here*" I am. To be able to hear God, we must recognize our own unworthiness and accept the forgiveness He alone can offer. Once forgiven of sin, we then have standing before God, through the shed blood of Christ, to hear from His Word (Hebrews 10:19) and to offer ourselves as a clean vessel for His use. "Hear" before "Here."

(September 8, 2011)

Hear Am I

"Here I am, Lord" in God's book I read,
    Isaiah spoke while upon his bed
His life he offered to God that day;
    What caused him though, these words to say?

"Here am I," Samuel one day spoke,
    When from his bed God had awoke.
What led this lad to commit his all
    And hearken to the Lord's soft call?

Both of these, many others, too,
    With yielded lives and eternal view
To hearken to the voice they heard
    Obedient to God's Holy Word.

How were they able these words to say?
    "Here am I," God's Word obey?
Insufficient men, no doubt,
    Yet through submission men devout.

What precept learned, what truth embraced,
    These runners applied to win their race?
This, then, is certain, one thing is clear,
    Before "Here am I" came "I will hear."

THIS MY PLEA

I wrote this poem as a song as I meditated on Psalm 32. Verse 8 says, "I will instruct thee and teach thee in the way which thou shalt go; I will guide thee with mine eye."

I left a good job in January 2012. I had no other job in line and the situation was heavy upon my family and me. I felt great relief (yet great turmoil) as I endeavored to place my trust in the Lord to provide new employment.

God did indeed meet our needs, and He provided a much better situation than my previous one. He is faithful! And the thought of the faithfulness of God presented so eloquently in Lamentations 3 is one that has comforted and sustained me throughout my Christian life. All He asks is that we, mortal flesh, trust Him! I do not know why that is so hard but sometimes it is, and yes, I do know why it is so hard—living in the flesh is the battle we face daily.

May God help us to walk in the Spirit and in submission to Him.

(January 17, 2012)

This My Plea

Walking on this journey, praying faithful I would be
    Yet within my heart the questions rise,
Do I take the path there, or do I stay the course
    Yearning that I may obtain the prize.

Guide me, oh, Thou Great Jehovah,
    Guide me so Thy voice be heard.
Help me in the choice before me,
    Guided by Thy Holy Word.

As I seek to live a holy life,
    A struggle of the old man with the new
One way, promised victory; one path sure defeat;
    Oh, Lord, may Your choice be my choice too.

As choices lie before me, I search within Thy Word,
    The way I must embrace becomes so clear:
The world shouts out directions, their path they'd have me take.
    But it's the still small voice of God that I must hear.

Knowing that the end I cannot see,
    Where this road will go and where I'll be,
And though my path may alter, and though my steps may falter,
    Help me, Lord, to constantly walk with Thee.
Holy Spirit, guide me… this my plea.

At the end, I'll look behind me… then I'll see…
    You were ever faithful, guiding me.

UNSAID, UNDONE

In late August 2012, I started experiencing severe shortness of breath with exertion. As a physician, I was aware this was a sign of cardiac ischemia. However, I had received a heart catheterization only two years earlier and had been told I had single-vessel coronary artery disease, "fixed" with a single stent. Since no one occludes his or her coronary vessels in two years, I was confident that I had only partially occluded my single stent.

In early September, God began increasing my symptoms. As these progressed, I started having thoughts that my time on earth was coming to an end. While driving from one of my ERs to another, I pondered my life and what I might present to God when I face Him.

The last stanza I wrote to reflect the suddenness of that meeting and the reality that if we are going to make changes in our lives, we need to make them immediately and without delay, because in the twinkling of the eye, we all could face our God!

Mercifully, God gave me extra days. At the end of September 2012, I underwent a five-vessel bypass because I had five completely occluded coronary vessels. My cardiologist related that with my proposed trip to Denver, Colorado, that was scheduled to occur in the beginning of October, I would not have survived the higher atmospheric pressure and lack of oxygen at that altitude. Merciful God, thank you for borrowed time.

(September 1, 2012)

Unsaid, Undone

Things unsaid and things undone,
　　And yet my race on earth is run.
Did I neglect a single thing
　　Ere to Him my talents bring?

From sin unspotted did I stand?
　　Or offer the fallen a helping hand?
Did my words nurture or destroy?
　　Was I the cause of stolen joy?

Was I humble, was I kind?
　　The good in others did I find?
Was I gentle, was I meek?
　　The face of God help others seek?

Did I falter when paths were dim,
　　Or did I trust and look to Him?

All these matters I yearn to know,
　　The answers ere my last breath go.
Futile though these questions bring
　　... for now I stand before my King.

CHOICE VESSELS

While reading in 2 Timothy 2, I came across the familiar verse 20, which speaks of the various vessels in a great house. As I meditated on that passage throughout the day, I considered what sort of vessel I was in the eyes of God. Was I a vessel that brought honor to God or did I dishonor Him through my behavior, spirit, or attitude?

That day, I had a visit to my home from my pastor, his wife, and a missionary, Dan Tessin. I was home recuperating from heart surgery only the week before. I was greatly encouraged that day as God spoke to my heart from His Word and through His servants. That evening I wrote this poem. I felt I was now living on borrowed time, yet in the third stanza, I spoke of investing our unborrowed time—the free choice of serving God out of a heart of love instead of requiring the chastening rod of God. May we be guided by the staff of God and not require the rod of God!

(October 1, 2012)

Choice Vessels

In every great house, there are vessels of gold
    And vessels of silver to honor the king
Within these same walls, there are vessels of wood
    And vessels of earth, which will dishonor bring.

Content in my sin I dishonor the King,
    Hid from the light of God's Word,
Deceiving myself and despising the truth,
    Resisting all that I've heard.

A vessel of gold I desire to be
    To honor my King is my quest,
Searching the scriptures His face I will seek
    With unborrowed time I'll invest.

Vessels of gold or vessels of wood
    The choice laid before us is clear
To honor our Father, or dishonor bring
    His voice, every morning, to hear.

ASLEEP

After my heart surgery in early October 2012, I evaluated my life to see where I needed to make change. One of the areas God revealed to me was that I needed to be a readier witness to strangers.

This poem was written after my devotional time on October 19, 2012. The third stanza reflected a thought God had given me and I meditated on that thought over and over after my surgery. "You were certain you had plenty of time, weren't you?" I wrote it from the perspective of the disciples who accompanied the Savior to the Garden of Gethsemane and who were completely unaware of the spiritual battle being waged all around them. Are you?

(October 19, 2012)

Asleep

Asleep was I while the Savior was praying
    Alone in the garden that night,
Asleep with others beside me,
    Unaware of the enemy's might.

Sleep was our deepest desire
    The day, long, and our flesh now so frail.
Unconcerned we had left our dear Savior,
    Alone as demons assail.

In slumber we passed through the evening
    Certain we had plenty of time
To accomplish the work He had given
    Though midnight the hour now chimed.

"Sleep on," the Savior admonished,
    Those words ring sad to this day.
For when we should have been watching,
    Instead on the ground we lay.

Do not judge my failure so quickly
    You, His commands who won't keep,
When winning the lost He desires
    Are you, like me, fast asleep?

THANKSGIVING

Thanksgiving has always been my favorite holiday. By nature, I am a thankful person. I am grateful, so very grateful, for what God has provided in my life.

Thanksgiving 2012, I was still recovering from heart surgery (although I had returned to work already), and as I sat at the dinner table and looked at my family, I became so profoundly grateful to God not only for His love and mercy, but also for the struggles He brings into our lives. It is the struggles that bring us so much closer to God *if we allow them to.*

That night, I wrote the words to this poem.

(Thanksgiving, 2012)

Thanksgiving

Thank You, Lord, for Your mercies true;
    For blessings, family, work to do.
But in my life bring into view
    That I must thank you for trials too.

In all struggles, thanks are due,
    For trials serve divine purpose too,
That through them sight might be anew
    To bring Your will in better view.

To focus thoughts that are askew
    That I'd be closer drawn to You.
This the treasure in them You knew,
    More grace You'll give to lead me through.

Photo Credit: Laura Veach

PRIDE

The great struggle in my life, when I am honest with myself, is the one against this great sin, pride. Although this poem is one of my shorter ones, the truth is very deep.

In early 2012, my pastor announced the title of a sermon he was contemplating preaching called "What Does Pride Look Like?" God used that sentence in my daily devotions to allow me to take my life apart and examine motives, actions, and thoughts. When my pastor finally preached the sermon (Pastor, remember, I love you) nearly six months later, it was almost anticlimatic because God had so worked me over during those six months that I was rightly aligned with Him on the matter.

Pride—the great hidden sin.

(December 18, 2012)

Pride

Battles fought and battles won
    Through the grace of God's own Son,
Yet if failure does abide,
    Attribute this to subtle pride.

Pride in secret ways and means
    In my life, not what it seems.
Quick to claim the glory of
    Things bestowed from God above.

Eager stating, "By my might,"
    Turning paths from day to night;
Wicked pride obscures God's ray
    And blocks the guidance of His way.

A STORY BEARS TELLING

I have often said that we must be careful whom we invite onto our boat. In the book of Jonah, the men who owned the boat Jonah traveled in found themselves in great turmoil because of the judgment of God on Jonah. Yet it was their stuff they had to throw overboard initially. A wrong decision about who you invite into your life can have disastrous effects, not only on your life, but also on those you love as well. You might find yourself throwing things from your life (peace, joy, time with God, etc.) overboard because of God's judgment on them.

God allowed me to read this book of Jonah one day with a humorous eye. How foolish we must look to God when we whimper and whine about wanting to do things our way and not His. Thankfully, God is a God of second chances... and third... and fourth. Indeed, while His patience is longsuffering, He is also a judge of unrepenting hearts and this is the lesson of Jonah to me.

(February 3, 2013)

A Story Bears Telling

A story bears telling
    Of a storm and men yelling,
When men failed to separate,
    For Jonah chose poorly,
Others suffered sorely
    And Jonah became fishing bait.

Yet it takes him three days
    Ere he kneels and prays
To be cast from the fish's mouth
    For he chose the wrong way.
When he started that day,
    He should have gone North and not South.

Through a fish and a worm
    Still his lesson unlearned.
Jonah whined and cried all that day,
    Fleeing the Lord
Yet loving a gourd,
    Jonah chose the selfish way!

Photo Credit: Jessica Veach

DIGGING UP A ROOT

In June of 2013, my pastor preached a series of four sermons on the sin of bitterness. He related that, in counseling hundreds of people, often sins had to be peeled back one by one until you come to the *root* of their sin. Often, this sin of bitterness against God or other people was the root sin.

I began to see, through his messages, that the sin of bitterness has deep roots. As a result of these deep roots, we too often only deal with the tips of the branches, thinking we have dealt with the root issue. Yet as time passes, another branch shoots out of the ground and exposes the fruit of our still undealt with bitterness. This is why the Bible, in Hebrews 12:15, says that the sin of bitterness, in troubling *you*, defiles *many* people. This sin in your life affects so many others! We must be diligent in digging up this root!

In contemplating these sermons after the fourth one, I wrote this poem on June 30, 2013.

(June 30, 2013)

Digging Up a Root

Don't peel my onion layers, Lord,
    Revealing things in my heart.
Overlook the root of bitterness
    On other issues start.

Tho' obedience is better than sacrifice
    My mask is sufficient for me,
My standing within the community
    Shouldn't that suffice for Thee?

The sin that separates us
    Must be something more;
My dress, my speech, my attitude,
    These must be the core.

The voice of God though speaks to me,
    "Submit to Truth, my son,
Confess this sin of bitterness
    If you want to commune as one."

With diligent inspection
    This root with eyes I now see
Must be stricken at the source,
    Ere my heart align with Thee.

So forgive me, Lord, of this my sin,
    To repent and return, my plea
Submitting my thoughts to Your control
    And my heart to refocus on Thee.

THE HARVEST

Autumn is the greatest time of the year... but I am a little biased. It brings back so many wonderful memories of important events in my life. Although I don't know a thing about farming, I love watching the crops being harvested as I travel the roads.

What a heartbreaking situation, however, when the crops are in need of harvesting in the face of an oncoming storm, and there are not enough workers. How much greater the heartbreak when viewed from a spiritual perspective. As the return of the Lord approaches, the opportunity to work in the Lord's field diminishes. God calls us to the field with growing urgency.

(November 14, 2013)

The Harvest

The Harvest is great, yet the laborers are few;
    Plenty of work for all still to do.
The Lord prayed for workers while the need greater grew,
    Yet in spite of the need, the field's missing you.

Moved with compassion, Christ bowed down in prayer
    That once blinded Christians this burden to bear.
Shaken from slumber, their eyes now aware
    To see the commission and ease their despair.

So throw off the slumber and commit to the cause
    The Lord will perfect what you see as your flaws,
To speak the word boldly without stutter or pause,
    Rescue lost souls from the wicked one's claws.

The Harvest is great, but few work the field
    Doing the will of the Father revealed.
He implores the Christian, ere their fate be sealed,
    The need is urgent, your heart you must yield.

Photo Credit: Rachel Veach

WHAT IT IS AND WHAT IT'S NOT

In 2014, my wife and I jokingly started using the phrase "It is what it is" as an explanation for nearly everything! When our kids, our friends, or our acquaintances would ask a "why" question, the inevitable response was "It is what it is."

We played around with this phrase for several months (and still occasionally resurrect it) until one of our children replied, "What if it's *not*?" That led to an addendum to our stock phrase: "It is what it is and not what it's not."

From that silliness came this more serious poem about the "Way that seemeth right unto a man" ("What it's not"), versus what the Bible says about salvation ("What it is").

The struggle since the creation of man is God's holy thoughts and way versus man's unholy human thoughts and ideas—and the two are opposed. Man has his own ideas of righteousness, and it certainly seems right (Proverbs 16:25) yet the end result is a sudden and swift destruction. God is not compromising about the way of salvation, but thankfully, He is long-suffering.

(April 2, 2014)

What It Is and What It's Not

Not the praise of the world I have sought,
    Not the victories in the fights I have fought,
Not the works of my hands I have wrought,
    But Heaven won by His blood I am bought.

It's not the praise of the crowd I have won,
    Not their laurels for the deeds I have done.
It's not the glory for the songs I have sung,
    But approval on the face of God's Son.

It's not the trials I face in my race,
    Not in my life if I leave here a trace,
Nor even in my walk if pride I abase,
    But rather am I saved by His grace.

It's not who I am or how I've been bred;
    It's not of me what men think or have said;
It's not my net worth when I fall dead;
    It's what's in my heart and not just my head.

So to truth, my friend, are you blind?
    Do the "rules" of religion tightly bind?
No peace or rest in your life do you find?
    It's to God's Word that your life must align.

It's what it is and what it is not,
    Not "being good" as you might have been taught,
Not going to church, though you know that you ought,
    But by His blood your soul must be bought.

THE SACRIFICE OF PRAISE

This phrase found in Hebrews 13:15 and Jeremiah 33:11 has come to mean a lot to Rachel and me. We titled our third CD after this because we desired that our voices would forever be raised in praise to God despite our circumstances, or rather maybe *because* of our circumstances. As I age, I have come to recognize that often greater praise is due God for Him *withholding* His hand in a matter sought than Him providing that which we longed for.

In the Old Testament, the sacrifice of praise offering (Hebrew: *Todah*) was a thank-you to God. There were two types of praise offerings in the law. One was a peace offering of an appropriate animal. It was never commanded but was a free will offering when one wanted to express great gratitude to a great God (this is found in Leviticus 3 and 7:11–21). The second offering was a vocal offering of singing God's praises. This is found throughout the psalms by King David, as well as Nehemiah 12:30, 31, 38, 40, 43, and is mentioned in Jeremiah 33:11.

Paul, the presumed writer of Hebrews, says in Hebrews 13:15 that we are to continue to offer the sacrifice of praise offering. However, not wanting to confuse the New Testament believer (after having just spent thirteen chapters saying Christ is the end of the Old Testament offering) he specifies which offering to continue. Not the animal sacrifice one, but the giving of praise from a grateful heart to a wonderful God.

(May 10, 2014)

The Sacrifice of Praise

Thank you, Lord,
    For all you've done,
For battles fought
    And victories won.
My voice I raise in earnest praise
    In gratitude throughout my days.

For what you've given
    And what you've not,
For things withheld,
    Though long I sought
Your faith remained in untold depths
    So often mined in faltering steps.

This sacrifice then I offer Thee
    A mind submitted in humility.
My will conformed, this heart obeys,
    My lips, the sacrifice of praise.

TIME SPENT IN PSALM 90

Psalm 90:9 says, "We spend our years as a tale that is told…" That phrase was beautiful to me. On June 3, 2014, I had this passage in my Bible reading. I was so struck by the words in this psalm, even though I had read it in the past countless times, that I had to read it aloud several times. For the next several days, I went back and reread this Psalm even though my Bible reading schedule had other passages I was to move on to. As I meditated on these words, God impressed several things to my heart—one of which was the brevity of time that is our lives.

I put words to my thoughts on June 6, 2014, and entitled the poem "Time Spent in Psalm 90" because of the repeated drawing by the Holy Spirit back to these verses. Each stanza is a reference to a verse in Psalm 90.

Time Spent in Psalm 90

We spend our years as a tale that is told
From the days of our youth till the time we are old.
We pass our hours in the eyes of our God,
Guided along by his staff and His rod.

As a watch in the night, our lives quickly pass.
We grow and we flourish, then wither as grass.
With sorrow and struggle our strength will not last.
As a flood on the earth, the waters flow fast.

May Thy glory appear to the eyes of our seed.
From the words of Thy book may forever they feed.
As we number our days, we'll rejoice and be glad,
For the days of affliction we doubtless have had.

The days of our years, perhaps threescore and ten,
Spent in labor and sorrow... but what happens then?
At eternity's edge our eyes lift to Thee
And our hearts cry in fullness, "FAITHFUL WAS HE!"

HERE I STAND

I had never been a pallbearer before or wore a cowboy hat, boots, and bolo tie… at least in public and especially never to a funeral! Yet all these were done in March 2015 for the funeral of Charles Massey.

Mr. Massey I had only known for four months but his life made an impact on mine. We were honored when he and his precious family were able to spend Thanksgiving 2014 with my family. In less than four months, he was ushered into the presence of his Savior.

After his graveside service, my daughters and I walked around the cemetery reading tombstones. The thought struck me that these markers stood, yet the dead could not. Nonetheless, one day I will stand before God, a sinner yet redeemed, forgiven, and clothed in new garments (Zechariah 3:1–5). While still in the cemetery, the words to this short poem were written on the back of an envelope. This poem is intentionally short for it is my hope that these words will be inscribed on my tombstone as a lasting testimony to God's grace.

(March 10, 2015)

Here I Stand

This marker stands, for I cannot,
    A man whose sins were one dark blot,
Yet heard I when the Savior sought,
    And now I stand my sins blood bought.

Condemned when in my flesh I stood,
    Works of my hands however good,
To purchase Heaven, never could
    Only by Faith whosoever would.

Photo Credit: Jessica Veach

THE BEST OF MEN

In 1 Peter 1:22–25, the Bible speaks of the frailty of the flesh and that the glory of man is as the flower of grass.

While in the air force, I had the opportunity to spend a number of months in Saudi Arabia in 1985. While there, I had the duty to run a medical clinic in Riyadh, the capital city, as well as travel to outlying posts around the country providing medical care. Assigned with me was a doctor who claimed to be a Christian and was described by his commanding officer as "the best of men." I saw this physician in Saudi Arabia spiral down into a wicked and decadent lifestyle when removed from his family. This phrase, "the best of men," turned over and over in my mind and come forth in this poem after I heard my pastor preach from this passage in 1 Peter. I saw that apart from a relationship with Christ and a passion for His Word, all we are, all we accomplish, all our dreams, as Paul put it, are nothing but dung. The best we are is still inadequate in God's eyes.

(April 8, 2016)

The Best of Men

The glory of man as the flower of grass
And soon it falleth away.
The best of us, the best we can be
Will not stand in eternity's day.

A self-made man is still made of man's self
Old nature, though polished to shine,
Corruptible still, and die yet it will
When man's branch is removed from the vine.

Denying atonement through His perfect blood
While exalting man's self-esteem
Blinded by Satan, man's eyes turn aside,
Rejecting God's will to redeem.

All flesh as grass will wither and fade,
As will man's thirst for praise.
These won't endure the onslaught of time
When exposed at the end of man's days.

For the best of men is still not enough
To purchase everlasting life.
The way of man, though it seemeth right,
Will result in destruction and strife.

The glory of man's wisdom doubtless will fade
For charisma burns fast as dross,
But the Power of God, His Holy Word
Shall never suffer loss.

So I admonish you, friend, embrace what is true,
Ere depart you this earthly sod
That wisdom and life and all that will last
Is found only in the Word of God.

MY SHEPHERD

I love the book of Jeremiah. While it records a tragic time in the history of Israel, a time of judgment from turning their back on God, it also speaks to the fact that God is faithful and will remember His people and will bless and restore as never before. While this restoration of Israel in present day is hinted at, it is miniscule compared to the full restoration God has planned for the nation. Israel will be restored to the position promised at the side of God and will rule the nations of Earth.

I was contemplating Jeremiah 31 on Father's Day 2015 (June 21) in a hotel in Spokane, WA, thousands of miles from my family. In this great chapter, God expresses His great love for His people in verse 3, "Yea, I have loved thee with an everlasting love." It was verse 10 of this chapter, however, which moved my heart to tears, "He that scattered Israel will gather him, and keep him, as a shepherd doth his flock."

It is no secret my precious wife loves sheep. It is by the grace of God and sheer fortitude of will that I have prevented her from turning our backyard into a pasture! She has a painting of a depiction of Christ cuddling a sheep. This thought, God's great compassion on the sheep of His pasture, moved me to tears, especially as I considered how quickly we, His sheep, wander away from Him (Isaiah 53). The way marks mentioned in verse 21 remind me of the ancient landmarks and the old paths God calls us to walk in.

This poem came quickly as I considered the merits of my Great Shepherd. The poem ends in reflection of verses 25 and 26. The thought moves me that God satisfies the sheep (Psalm 23) satiates the weary soul, replenishes the sorrowful, and provides sweet rest. The final line has application to rest He provides at the end of a hard day, but more importantly (and, to my point), refers to the close of our earthly days, when He gives us the rest promised in Hebrews 4:9, 10. Amen!

(June 21, 2015)

Photo Credit: Jonathan Veach

My Shepherd

The Lord who scatters will gather in
As a shepherd doth his flock.
He shall guard, defend each one
In the crevice of the Rock.

My Lord, the Tower, Salvation Strong,
And His wings a shelter sure,
His Words refresh and feed the soul,
Offering rest and water pure.

He the Fount of waters deep
That my soul is longing for,
As the deer pants for the brook
May I crave Your Word the more.

My soul a watered garden, fresh,
Ransomed from the dark of night
Your mercy shed upon my heart
Your burden easy, Your yoke light.

Thou the Shepherd of my heart
By my side the paths we trod,
Correct my steps O Staff of God
And not require the chastening rod.

Waymarks heaped upon the way
Remind me to return once more,
As a sheep who wanders far
Shepherd, true, my soul restore.

Gently led You through my days
At break of morn when I arise.
In fellowship found sweet retreat
And in peace You'll close my eyes.

CHOOSE THIS DAY

The Christian life is a life of choices. Life choices, daily choices, even moment-by-moment choices. Will you listen in a particular moment to the Holy Spirit and submit to Him (James 4:6, 7), or will you respond to a situation in anger, frustration, self-will, or pride? This is the essence of the Christian life: choosing each moment to walk in submission to the Holy Spirit.

Much of the Bible reflects this theme of choosing. Very obvious are the choices presented by Elijah atop Mt. Carmel (serve God or Baal) and Joshua at the close of his life ("choose ye this day whom ye will serve... "). More subtle, however, are the thousands of New Testament references to choosing reflected in the words *let, may, yield,* and many others. The writers offer options and often cite the consequences for choosing poorly. For example, 2 Peter 3:18 says we are to grow in grace and knowledge. It is the Christian's choice to grow... or not.

My pastor, using this text along with 2 Timothy 3:14–17, preached a Sunday morning sermon on June 28, 2015, entitled "The Learning Process of the Christian." He spoke on the choice to walk in faith or walk by sight and the choice to develop a passion for the Word of God. This struck a chord with me as I contemplated the doctrine of two paths taught throughout scripture. By that evening, this poem was written.

(June 28, 2015)

Choose This Day

Thy Word a lantern to my feet
A light unto my path,
In its pages there I found
Salvation from Thy wrath.

To search It daily, this my quest
And to Thy way submit,
To grow in grace and knowledge too
For this is true profit.

If wisdom lack, it's offered there,
Your Word says I must ask,
Request in Faith and waver not
The "Walk by Faith" our task.

This Walk by Faith few understand
The "Walk by Sight" most choose.
In pride they walk, submitted not
God's fellowship they lose.

So where the source of faith in God?
This Fount of waters, deep?
This walk by faith He calls us to
Requires you wake from sleep.

Your doubts and fears and lack of trust
Must cast, you, at His feet.
Your heart you must submit in trust
Ere joy supplant defeat.

Why hesitate, then, at the brink
Half-hearted serve your Lord?
Choose now this day and waver not
This walk by faith secured.

Plunge in whole heart and take that step
Give God your last reserve.
For soon you'll bow before His throne
And face the One you served.

You'll give account for all you've done
And things you did not do.
"Why didn't you trust me more, my child?"
You'll hear Him say to you.

"Did you not think I'd meet your needs,
And give you victories won?"
You'll weep when this He'll say to you
"I cannot say 'well done.'"

TWO DISCIPLINES

In Matthew 7:24, God will liken the man who hears the saying of Christ and does them as a wise man. These are the two disciplines: to hear and do. To hear without doing is not a true disciple of Christ, and this man is called a fool in verse 26. To do without hearing is to operate without the Spirit of God in control in your life. Unfortunately, this is the state of most religions and we see it in many "good" churches. Many are so caught up with activity and "doing" that the children turn eighteen and walk away because they were never taught to have a real relationship with Christ. In place of that essential part of their spiritual life, they were provided a cacophony of activity; within the church, they were taught to live for their lusts.

This poem came rapidly after hearing my pastor preach a sermon on the source of wisdom, using Luke 8 (the soils of the sower) and Matthew 7 as his texts.

(July 5, 2015)

Two Disciplines

The next right step
(This path is clear)
Is made each day
When I choose to hear.

The road before
Is laid out to me
The choice I take?
To be of use to Thee.

The soil of my heart
When I hear Thy Word
Is to conform my life
To the words I heard.

But hearing alone
Is only partly true
For God expects
Me to hear AND do.

By obeying His Word
In the choices I make
More effective I'll be
For eternity's sake.

These two disciplines
Either one, alone,
Brings dishonor to God
Because you have not grown.

So hear AND do
Each our choice this hour
Embrace them BOTH
And so walk in Power!

WALK IN LOVE

God calls us to love one another. It's a commandment, not a suggestion. Quite frankly, this is sometimes so very difficult to do because, well, people are sometimes as lovable as porcupines! Yet God calls us to love one another. It's easy to love the lovable. But the unlovable? How can God expect us to do that? How is that possible?

It actually is very simple. Too often, we try to act out the Christian life in our own power. Sometimes we are successful, at least to the eyes of the world. But in God's eyes, living the Christian life in the flesh is an utter failure and mocks the Holy Spirit. What God desires in our life is to learn to submit to the Holy Spirit moment by moment and especially in times of spiritual impact. This is a principle I learned from my pastor—to turn things over to God and thereby submit to the Holy Spirit and respond as He would desire us to at the point of impact. Thereby (and only then) we are submitted and obtain God's help in our lives. To refuse to submit is simply pride—and God resists you (see James 4:6–11). Not just does not listen but actively resists you! I don't want that in my life! Walk in love!

Written July 5, 2015 while reading 1 John 4:7–8.

Walk in Love

This commandment of God
"Let us love one another"
Is written in His Word
And given to every brother.

For His love is shown
Within our lives
Only when we submit
In the moment Satan tries.

Beloved, let us love one another.

If we live through Him
As He commands us to
Our love is on display
For the world to view.

While we're called to live
Separated from sin
If we walk kindly
Then a brother we'll win.

Beloved, let us love one another.

Walk in love and light
Let your lamp never dim
In your gentle walk
You will serve to honor Him.

For in submitting to God
We respond in love
Not reacting in flesh
But filled from above.

Hear His voice today
And so walk in love
Better order your steps
As He speaks from above.

Beloved, let us love one another.

GOD'S PROGRAM

We are living in an apostate age, much of it the result of "programs" promoted by well-meaning churches. God's plan from the beginning of time has not changed. His people, His sheep, hear His voice, and follow Him. God spoke in the beginning face-to-face with man, then through select men, then through prophets and finally, through His perfect and completed Word. And His plan for two thousand years has been simple: the Holy Spirit would convict, reprove, correct, and instruct through the reading/hearing of the Word of God; men would repent and submit to God, empowered to live a holy life by the Spirit of God. This is God's program.

But man's plan has usurped God's plan in most churches and the result is the anemic Christian we see today. Man's plan has been to turn the church into a well-designed machine with unending activities, contests, circus acts, and sensual music performances more conformed to the world's style than scriptural holiness. People do not live lives submitted to the Holy Spirit but, rather, live their Christian life in self-righteousness.

To whom was God speaking in Revelation 3:14–22 if not to this current age? I am convinced most churches could continue on into the Tribulation period without any noticeable change because they have operated for many years apart from the Holy Spirit.

This poem was written after hearing my pastor preach a sermon entitled "God's Program is the Word of God."

(July 12, 2015)

God's Program

A heart's desire for change
As God would have you to
From the written Word of God
The Spirit calls to you.

Flee from sin, resist your lust,
Humble 'neath God's hand
Why dabble all ye in the world
And follow sin's demand?

Repentance is the path to take
Repentance from your sin
Repentance of your fleshly ways
Repentance- where you begin.

Most men are taught to live for self
And submit not to God's Word,
Yet that is where the Spirit speaks
The voice of God there heard.

Conform your ways to scripture now
For then God will you approve,
For this submission is God's plan
To develop God's world view.

A student of God's Word is then
Important so you'll mature;
To it God calls you to align
And fellowship assure.

God's program is the Word of God
Not entertainment, music thrill,
Not circus tricks or activities,
But His Word your life to fill.

The foolishness of preaching is
The wisdom of God's plan,
The beauty of God's Word proclaimed
By God's chosen man.

Humble NOT and be devoured
This your choice to make;
God is true to His own Word
Why must your life He break?

Choose to follow ways of truth
God's way to not obstruct
Pernicious ways the other choice
Through it a swift destruct.

So submit ye then to Holy Writ
For this is wisdom true,
Humbled 'neath the Mighty Hand
For THERE is safety for you.

Photo Credit: Vonda Murdock

RISE ABOVE

Psalm 119:4–16 speaks of the need to meditate on the Word of God rather than just reading the Bible. Certainly, reading the Bible is advantageous to our lives, but many do this in a mechanical way without meditation on the verses, never giving the Spirit of God an opportunity to speak to their heart. This is where real change occurs in one's life.

I knew a man once who publicly boasted of the number of chapters he had read in the Bible each week. He would often stand in church and give a "testimony" of how far he read that week. Yet his life was characterized by a broken marriage, broken fellowship with his children, and a reputation for being mean-spirited. I often wondered if he had allowed God time to speak to his heart as he read. I suspect not.

The discipline of listening to the Spirit of God, of awaiting His still small voice, of meditating on scripture, cannot be over-emphasized. Yet I fear it is becoming a waning practice, especially in America. We simply lead too busy a life to have time to "wait on God". In this age of microwaved everything, we want our time with God to be quick and bullet-pointed as well. We crave entertainment instead of doctrine and sermonettes filled with stories rather than calls to personal holiness.

For our lives to change, God's Word must be real to us as we develop our relationship with Christ.

(July 19, 2015)

Rise Above

Precious Thy Words when I meditate,
Not just words I read in a book;
When applied to my life as I ponder them,
Their relevance I'll not overlook.

The difference between just reading Your Word
And hiding it deep in my heart
Is my intent to Thy precepts as I read line by line
That from my sin against Thee depart.

A forgetful hearer has not hidden Thy Word
His walk, a mechanical one;
A facade of religion sufficeth to him
His intent? To get reading done.

But God has a purpose for His perfect Word
In the Spirit to read it each day,
To rise above reading, on it meditate
For only then, will you His precepts obey.

SIMPLE TRUTH

As I contemplate the simplicity of the gospel, I marvel at how men have tried to complicate its simplicity. When I make an acquaintance with members of "religions" and cults, I enjoy asking them to explain their system of beliefs. Sometimes, the answers I get are so convoluted and estranged from scriptural truth that the blinding of their eyes by Satan is obvious. Others, while their beliefs contain some truth (as any lie does), their commitment is to something other than stated truth from the scripture. Some are convinced that church practice supersedes revealed truth in scripture; others hold visions and dreams as superior to God's Word.

I consider this to be a fulfillment of 2 Timothy 4:1–4 and a sign of the end times. Clearly, although doctrine is in an elevated position in scripture, in an apostate age many push it aside as unimportant. Some even dismiss it in preference to "unity."

I wrote this poem following a discussion with a member of a cult as I discussed the simplicity of the gospel.

(July 26, 2015)

Simple Truth

The truth that comes with simplicity
Is easy to be understood,
But a veil is pulled over simple truth
As only wicked men would.

For these would blind a seeker's heart
And draw his focus away
From wisdom within the Word of God
And to fables be led astray.

A rewarder of those who submit to Him
God offers the humbled His grace
In faith they trust His promises,
Empowered they run life's race.

But this simple truth men try to obscure
Who claim in the flesh they can serve,
Angry, impatient, frustrated they walk
A reap to the flesh they deserve.

Simple truth from God's Word then is this:
Confess and repent every day,
Spend time in the Word and in fellowship,
Submit to the Spirit, and pray.

A TROPHY OF GRACE

One of the great joys of my life is sitting talking with my precious wife about spiritual matters. One day in July 2015, we were talking about our amazement that God would use any of us in service to Him, given the scars in our lives. This conversation led to another and my wife used the term "a trophy of His grace." That thought stuck with me and within several days, I had written this poem.

This poem reflects the wonder we felt as we considered His holiness and our unworthiness. I was overwhelmed, as the second stanza relates, that my past was not just speckled with sin but, before the eyes of a Holy God, it was bathed in sin… yet He still sought me out to save me. What a Great Savior!

(July 27, 2015)

A Trophy of Grace

A Trophy of Grace, how can this be?
That God would consider a sinner like me
And see something worthy that I could not see
To fashion a vessel of honor for Thee.

My past, not speckled, but buried in sin
That God with me a new life would begin
And cleanse from my shame, without and within
All this, and yet further, eternity win.

When I think of the things in my life which bring shame
An outcast and exiled, my self sole to blame
As a leper in scripture, I was the same
Like the beggars and poor, the blind and the lame.

He took this clay, broken, and fashioned anew
Each piece situated where only He knew
And washed out the inside, from His fountain He drew
Pure water, the Spirit, His presence to view.

How can this flesh give adequate praise?
A sinner redeemed from Hell's fiery blaze
From the trash heap of life, Your mercy did raise
A Trophy of Grace for eternity's days.

MY ABCS

This poem came from a sermon my pastor preached on August 2, 2015. His points, I thought, were intriguing as he mentioned the need to mature in Christ. "A" was for *attitude*, "B" for *behavior*, and "C" for how you *communicate*.

Perhaps the greatest hindrance in a Christian's life is the control of their thought life. The lack of control in that area affects so many other areas that a godly walk is not possible without it. Behavior is a critical area as well but is, too often, under control of the flesh. Even good behavior, if it is maintained in the flesh, is an ungodly thing… and very exhausting. Behavior—our responses, reactions, interactions—needs to be under the Spirit's control. Communication needs to be Spirit controlled as well. A bad look, a frustrated sigh, rolled eyes, all communicate that you are not being Spirit controlled. While you may not curse someone, you are still operating in the flesh and in this way are not pleasing to God.

So the ABCs are a critical barometer of where you are in your Christian walk. This poem was written to try to convey those points.

(August 2, 2015)

My ABCs

As a young child I went to school
My ABCs to learn,
Enabling me to read and write
From childish things to turn.

A natural thing, this change in me
As knowledge in me grew,
From reading books on Dick and Jane
To those on science I flew.

But as a Christian, I ponder this thought:
Is growth expected of me?
What does God require in life?
I ask Him on bended knee.

He answered me that, as a child,
I learned my ABCs,
I must learn anew these rules
If Him I'd ever please.

The "A" is where this change begins
For this is Attitude.
How you think, controlling thoughts?
Pure or on things crude?

The "B" is for Behavior, yours
It speaks to how you act.
Are you walking worthy in Christ,
Or the Spirit's power lack?

"C" is Communication, true
The sighs, the looks, your speech
Have you seasoned it with grace
In kindness others reach?

God desires that you grow up
Submit to Him your will
Controlled in mind, in mouth, in walk,
These, by the Spirit fill.

So learn the ABCs, my friend
The rules of a Godly walk,
How to think and behave, too
And how, as a Christian, talk.

AMAZING GRACE

I am amazed at God's grace, especially as I look at my life and how undeserving I know I am. I started this poem fifteen years ago and quit after writing the first six lines. As I looked through my notebook of unfinished poems, I came across this one. As I pondered God's grace, the words came quickly, and within a matter of minutes, this poem was written. There clearly is no better word for God's grace than *amazing*!

(August 6, 2015)

Amazing Grace

Amazing Grace, its depths untold
That God would accept me and His arms would enfold.
Undeserved merit, to a heart that was cold
Unworthy, yet invited to approach the throne bold.

Amazing Grace, so costly yet free
His mercy extended to a sinner like me
That He would hang on an undeserved tree
Only His blood, the guilty man's plea.

Amazing Grace, no man ere could know
How the creator of all, to a wooden cross go
Displaying compassion, to a world mercy show
And allow at man's hands, His precious blood flow.

Amazing Grace, my sin did erase,
Removed it completely and left not a trace.
I'll weep at His Throne, having finished my race
In awe of my Savior's... Amazing Grace.

OVERHAUL ME, LORD

In 1998, I wrote a list of things that were "messed up" on my car at the time. I set that list aside in a notebook and came across that list in 2015, seventeen years later. I chuckled as I reviewed the list because I had written at the bottom of that list, "Would a tune up even help?"

In August 2015, I was driving to an ER in Helena, AR, when I saw an old car in a field just off the highway. My thoughts went to a dear friend of our family, Tony DiFlorio, who (as a great mechanic) I thought could probably fix that car and make it beautiful. One thought flowed to another and I recalled the list I had written seventeen years before. It is an amazing thing how in the hands of a master mechanic an old clunky car can be beautiful and useful again. Likewise, in the hands of the Almighty God, a broken down life, cast aside by most, can be restored and useful once again to the Savior.

That same day, I wrote this poem and have dedicated it to my mechanic friend, Tony DiFlorio.

(August 6, 2015, Dedicated to Tony DiFlorio, my friend)

Photo Credit: Jonathan Veach

Overhaul Me, Lord

Lord, I need an overhaul, a tune up will not do,
I'll bring myself to Your garage, to be checked out by You.

I've got a lot of things to fix, I'll list them one by one,
I think I'll sit and wait on You, until they all get done.

First of all, the engine needs work, my power seems so weak;
I've labored in the flesh so long, Your strength, Lord, I must seek.

My headlights don't seem to shine too far, my vision's gotten dim,
Perhaps within God's Word I'll find, a lighted path from Him.

The gas tank needs a cleaning out (the world's sugar was poured in);
This vessel needs a thorough wash, purged of all its sin.

The cooling system's all messed up, it overheats when under pressure;
For things little seem to aggravate, far beyond due measure.

My steering needs alignment too, for I often veer afield,
I need to walk in old paths shown, control I need to yield.

An oil change is critical, fresh oil an urgent need,
Submission to the Spirit of God, Your commandments I must heed.

The spark plugs need to be changed out, revival spark they lack
For when Your power is needed most, I seem to just hold back.

The muffler is very bothersome, like a hateful tongue clangs on
Settle this noisy instrument, make the anger that drives it gone.

The taillights just don't function, Lord, others don't seem to see,
My beacon must be very faint, they don't see You in me.

Finally, Lord, the turn signal's broke, but leave that if You will,
So I'll not turn aside from You, and stay the straight path still.

TIME WELL SPENT

In my devotions on August 7, 2015, God spoke to me about how critical and essential the time was that I spent with Him. This poem was written that same day to reflect the impression He made on my heart.

The Bible speaks a lot on pride. Perhaps the most proud man is the man who refuses to submit his life to God. This is lived out in the life of the man who chooses to live independent from God. He never spends time with God in fellowship, he won't seek God's face and direction in decisions, and he refuses to submit to the Holy Spirit in time of spiritual impact but instead responds in the flesh. This man is double minded and will not receive anything from God (James 1:5–8). In addition, because he has an unsubmitted heart, God actively resists him (James 4:6–10).

All of this could be avoided with a quiet time with God. This is the time where I ask God to examine my heart and reveal any unconfessed sin in my life; where I submit my life to truth taught in the scripture; where I seek His guidance for my day. This is a holy time and is precious to me. It is time well spent.

(August 7, 2015)

Time Well Spent

From this holy place, oh, God,
May I never choose removal,
Always searching in Thy Word
That I may win approval.

Hearing what the Word of God
Speaketh to my spirit
Longing for Thy presence, Lord,
Though sin would cause me fear it.

Help me hear the Words You speak
And for knowledge I implore
That holiness might be the cause
And lust would lose allure.

Unhurried time I'll spend with You
In fellowship so sweet
Sanctify this time, oh, God,
My place of safe retreat.

Treasured time within Thy book,
As we converse alone
The Spirit teaching me in truth
As I come before Thy throne.

So thank You, God, for this holy time
As my will to Yours is bent
Where I may see You face-to-face
And for this time well spent.

THE UNSTABLE MAN

I wrote "Time Well Spent" nine days before I wrote this poem. If you will see the "back story" to that poem, you will see I reference the unstable man in that poem.

I don't think it a coincidence that nine days later my pastor preached from James 1:3–8 about the unstable man. As he began preaching, I had to laugh because this was exactly what God had shown me the week before in impressing upon me the essential nature of the quiet time with God.

The doubled minded man speaks of faith but does not practice it. The cords mentioned in the first stanza refer back to Proverbs 5:22 and describe the sins we won't confess as ropes which bind us.

I wrote this poem on the drive home from church, so ready was my heart to hear the words of the sermon.

(August 16, 2015)

The Unstable Man

Double minded and never established,
Who talk of faith but walk in flesh,
Living a life of emotional bondage
The cords that bind each day they refresh.

Unstable this man in all his ways
A life given over to lust.
Self-righteous he lives, apart from Thy Word
He lives never learning to trust.

God's Word can cleanse the darkest of sins,
No heart too black to be pure,
Regardless of scars obtained in the past,
Repentance provideth a cure.

Double minded to walk in flesh not in faith,
You'll receive from the Lord not a thing,
As a wave of the sea, you are driven by wind,
On you and your family destruction you bring.

God calls you repent from this unstable bent
To seek Him on bended knee.
Take hold of this fact, if wisdom you lack
So unstable no longer you'll be.

MANGER KING

I had started this poem fifteen plus years ago with the first six lines and had set it down. As I leafed through my "poetry notebook" of unfinished poems, I picked this one out, and within several days, the words came to complete it. It is sad to me that crass commercialism has usurped the simplicity of Christmas. It must grieve our Savior that Christians get so caught up in the buying frenzy and take their eyes off their manger King.

(August 21, 2015)

Manger King

This time of year, we offer praise
At the birth of God's own Son
The gate to heaven open wide
The path His blood has won.

This child born a man though God
By Angels then proclaimed
Within your heart God's true desire
He'd become your Savior named.

In ancient times this Babe was born
The wise men gifts did bring
They bent their knees and bowed their hearts
And honored Him as King.

Many years have come and gone
Since this Babe was born
Some still see Him as a child
His message proudly scorn.

They exchange gifts and celebrate
The season they know not
They cross Christ out of Christmas
Without a second thought.

But soon one day they'll understand
And regret this very thing
They'll see Him not a tiny babe
But in majesty their King.

THE INWARD REBEL

My pastor was preaching on a subject completely unrelated and mentioned that he was writing a booklet on the "Anatomy of a Rebel" and how some rebels are rebels inwardly and look like "normal Christians" outwardly.

This started a train of thought as I pondered rebels who didn't look the part in scripture. Several men came to mind but none more so than the prodigal's brother. He harbored a root of bitterness likely all the years his brother was in the far country. It was fully revealed in his refusal to come to the celebration for the prodigal.

As an inward rebel, he still obeyed the father and still worked the fields, yet can you imagine his thoughts on how, in his opinion, his father had mishandled the situation with the prodigal?

Sometimes, the inward rebel is in greater danger than the outward one for they are content to remain estranged from God yet pretending to be right with Him. These are those upon whom Christ pronounced the woes as hypocrites.

(September 7, 2015)

The Inward Rebel

How does an inward rebel appear?
A rebel who looks not the part.
He'll appear to see and hear the truth
But within has an ungodly heart

He'll appear to walk upright in truth
And continue to do as he's told.
He'll carry his Bible and speak of God
But to Christ his heart remains cold.

He'll point to others with a fault
And inside accuse them to God,
Yet will fail to see his sin deep within
His phylacteries he will make broad.

He'll listen but he will not hear.
He'll see yet blind will remain,
But outwardly he'll still look the part;
The Christian walk he will feign.

The Prodigal son, a perfect example;
Though TWO lived within that home
One who stayed, yet seethed within
The other left there to roam.

One, an outward rebel, for sure
The other, an inward one
One who left to fulfill his lust,
But the other? An unthankful son.

So how does the inward rebel appear?
To define it, this is the essence:
He wants the things the Father can give
But he does not want His presence.

COME YE OUT

In my devotions one morning (September 12, 2015) I read in Hosea of his love for his wife, Gomer, and how God used his experience to demonstrate His own relationship with Israel. In my study of this passage, I used J. Vernon McGee's commentary and read where he said that many churches are like brothels. As I pondered that, I realized the truth to that statement. No longer does doctrine dominate the teaching in our churches. Instead, charisma, excitement, entertainment, activities, and showmanship have reigned supreme.

People think they are honoring God when they yell, run the aisles, scream, and even shout "amen" loudly but do not realize that much of that is in the flesh. Churches can teach their people to follow their flesh, and as a result, these churches are "exciting" but there is no real spiritual change in people.

I grow weary of preachers who scream, rant, throw things, and the like, yet are not submitted to the Spirit in their life. Their marriages are often disasters, anger rules their lives, and their children's hearts are stolen by the world as a result. We entertain the young with puppet shows, carnivals and "spiritual vignettes," yet do not teach them how to have a real relationship with God. All the while patting ourselves on the back because we had "hundreds say the sinner's prayer" yet are never seen again. These are brothels, dressed up as churches, because they promote adulterous spiritual behavior.

(September 12, 2015)

Come 'Ye Out

Many churches are run as a brothel,
Unfaithful to God and His Word
Unfaithful, though expressing devotion
Yet denying the truth, are unstirred.

Denying a bloody atonement,
That the Savior is God in the flesh,
That the Lord still requires repentance
Itching ears yearn for something that's fresh.

As Hosea redeemed his wife, Gomer
From a brothel of man, deep in sin
These the Savior desires to rescue
The sincere who are searching for Him.

So the church that is run as a brothel
With entertainment replaces the truth
Dulls the senses, removes Godly doctrine
With activities hypnotize youth.

"Come ye out from them," calls the Savior.
"Turn again to Me with your heart,
I'll betroth thee in mercy and kindness,
From your side I will never depart."

"Come ye out from them," calls the Master.
"Unfaithful no longer to be,
To My Word renew your devotion,
And My mercy I'll shower on thee!"

A HERITAGE OF FAITH

Our family reunion in Gatlinburg, TN, in September 2015 was a very special time. Each of my brothers and sisters and members of their families gathered for a week of great fun and fellowship.

On Sunday, September 13, we gathered together, more than thirty of us, and praised God for His mercy and grace to us and for the godly heritage He had given us. Our discussion centered on Christ and His working in our families and in the lives of our mother and father, now long deceased.

Several days later, I had to fly to Florida for a brief business meeting. On the flight, my mind went back to that service. By the time I landed in Ft. Lauderdale, I had written this poem.

(September 16, 2015)

Photo Credit: Public Domain

A Heritage of Faith

The gift of faith, a heritage pure
Many would give any price
    But a gift of fine gold
    Is precious to hold
And came at great sacrifice.

First, a Savior who was willing to die
His life on a rugged cross gave
    Though His mercy so deep
    By the lost counted cheap
But our parents to Calvary clave.

Then, a father who understood work
Countless hours in labor he spent
    In the heat and the cold.
    Though arms growing old
No complaints, in pain his back bent.

Then a mother, true keeper at home
Who did what few could have done
    Many hours on knees
    The Savior to please
To Christ, saw all her kids won.

This heritage, then, was costly to give
All these, empowered from above
    A Savior, a father
    A sweet Godly mother
Gave, and expressed their great love.

But alas, in scripture, we also can read
Of a generation who knew not the Lord
    Could this future portend
    And our Godly line end
And our Savior no longer adored?

So serve ye the Savior with passion
Submit to God's Spirit in you
    Walk with God every day
    So your generations will say,
"I want Him to be my Savior too."

THE SCORNER

The Bible speaks of scorners frequently and never in a good light. They are described as people who will not hear instruction, who can't take correction, and who cannot find wisdom no matter how hard they search because they refuse the Wisdom of God. Their end is not a pleasant one, as they will be consumed or destroyed.

Over several months, my pastor had alluded to scorners in various messages, usually with a one or two line comment. This poem is a reflection of those comments as I contemplated the arrogance and pride of a person who considered himself wiser than God.

(October 4, 2015)

The Scorner

Walking through life with a chip on your shoulder
A fight just waiting to start
A spirit of anger, arrogance, pride
The issue, my friend, is your heart.

Demanding perfection in all who you meet
(A standard you'll not hold yourself to)
Apt to accuse, though godly you look
While your root of bitterness grew.

Acknowledging not the grace you are shown
Nor kindness, given freely by others
You, a scorner, of holy things are
And strife you stir among brothers.

How long will you still follow this path?
In anger, a fist raised to God?
Your service and offerings rejected by Him
You abide 'neath His chastening rod.

Wisdom God gives in His Word for your life
Obey Him or destruction you'll see
This spirit you have is not of the Lord
And repentance the one remedy.

Repent, God says, of this ungodly walk
Repent of the venom you spew
Great harm you have done, and souls left unwon
In Hell, will doubtless scorn you.

OF JUDGMENT

While reading in 1 Peter 4:14–19, I came to the realization that as American Christians we have a dim view of suffering. We often view it as a punishment from God rather than, as the Word of God describes it, a path to exceeding joy. We have no real appreciation for the suffering the average "third- world" Christian undergoes on a daily basis.

I had an acquaintance many years ago who once publically requested prayer because of their "intense suffering." When he explained it further, the foundation of his suffering was "persecution" in the work place because he wanted to have a full sized Christmas tree beside his desk and his bosses said "no." He was willing to carry this to the highest court in the land—for this silliness.

Much of our "suffering" occurs from our own stupidity because we have not sought direction from the Holy Spirit.

May God help us to judge our lives and seek to glorify God in our daily walk. And if we suffer, may it be for godliness.

(October 5, 2015)

Of Judgment

If judgment begins at the house of God
Do we, as His children, obey?
Is our walk submitted to divine control?
Does He direct what we say?

If the righteous are saved by the grace of God
What shall the ungodly do?
Who choose to resist the cords of love,
Are they influenced by you?

We can suffer for evil or suffer for good
The choice to be godly is yours
If you suffer for evil your heart is not right
But for good, His grace He outpours.

When we stand before His judgment seat
Will we, at that time, be ashamed?
Were our motives pure? Did we honor Him?
Or by men want our deeds proclaimed?

But when the sinner stands before the Great White Throne,
Having rejected the Savior's plea
The words they'll hear will echo through time
"Unforgiven, depart from me."

HUMBLE

Everything about Christ's earthly ministry reflects humility. As I read the Christmas story in Luke 2:1–35, I was overcome of His great humility demonstrated in every facet of His life. He was born humbly, the creator of the universe. He walked humbly, having no possessions save for His raiment. His trial was a humble affair as He allowed the creation to smite the creator. With just a look, He could have executed His fierce vengeance, but he chose to remain humble. His death was humble as he submitted Himself to the will of man.

The concept of humility is often misunderstood. Many think it means you have to debase yourself and think you are lower than a worm in order to be humble. The scriptures teach that true humility is just a submission of yourself to another's will. James 4 speaks of this humility—of submitting ourselves to God at the point of spiritual impact—and it is this submission which allows the power of God to be evident in our lives. To refuse to humble ourselves in this manner demonstrates we are prideful and seek to live independent from God, as if we are saying, "I can do this in my own strength; I don't need your help, God." This is the true definition of pride, living independent from God, and this invites God's active resistance in our life (James 4:6–8).

(December 20, 2015)

Humble

A humble birth in manger lay
In a lowly cattle stall,
How could He choose this pauper's birth
And not a palace hall?

A humble walk, a meager fare,
He walked with common man.
Clothed was He in humility
To reveal redemption's plan.

A humble trial, falsely accused
Yet spoke He not a word.
The jeers and mocking of the crowd
Were all my Savior heard.

A humble death, a borrowed tomb
No monument He sought
That through this lowly path by God
Salvation's plan was brought.

Exalted now in Heav'n above
At God's right hand is He
The path for man to come to Him
Is through humility.

The humble birth, walk, trial, and death
My Savior did embrace,
For only to the humbled man
Will God give of His grace.

So how can man approach the Lord
His righteousness appease?
His mercy, favor, and His grace
Are found on bended knees.

THE LIGHT

In Matthew 2:1–12, the story of the wise men is told as they followed God's star to Bethlehem. God will likely not place another star in the sky to guide us today as He did two thousand years ago but has provided a more perfect and specific light to guide our daily walk in the Word of God (Psalm 119:105).

Additionally, the light God uses today to bring others to Him is this same light, shared by fallible men (Romans 10:14–17). We have no light in and of ourselves, but as we walk in fellowship with God, He cleanses us from sin so His light shines in us. (1 John 1:5–7). As we walk with God, we merely reflect God's light to others. The light does not originate with us any more than the moon's light originates apart from the sun. When sin is in our life, our light is darkened.

On December 23, 2015, our pastor preached a sermon on the light of Christmas. One particular verse, Proverbs 13:14, really struck a chord with me. It is quoted in the first two lines. The rest of the poem formed rather quickly from there.

(December 23, 2015)

The Light

The law of the wise is a fountain of life
To depart from the snare of death,
Neglect of its counsel, a foolhardy thing,
You'll regret to your last living breath.

To allow your bible to sit idly by
Not lighting your steps every day
Is the path into sin and destruction begin
As you stumble on your unlighted way.

A Christian is called to walk in the light
"How is this done?" you may say,
Confessing your sin each day you begin
And fellowship in His Word every day.

So help me, Oh, Lord, in this quest every day
That my ear to your voice would align,
Your light I might see and useful I'd be
So through me, on others, you'd shine.

THE WAY OF MAN

The Bible, very clearly and in multiple places, speaks of the concept of two paths. When I preach (I often preach at a local nursing home as an outreach of our local church) I frequently quote this passage in Proverbs 16:25, "There is a way that seemeth right unto a man but the end thereof are the ways of death."

The Bible speaks of only one path to Heaven and it courses through the blood of Christ. Jesus, in John 14:6, explained that He was the door to God. Yet men explain this away and claim many paths to God. These are the ways of men and are a deceitful pursuit, which will end in death.

This poem speaks of the one true path to God, through Jesus Christ.

(December 27, 2015)

The Way of Man

There is a way which seemeth right to a man
But the end are the ways of death.
Too late he discovers this truth of God
Shortly after his last earthly breath.

He's trusted in things that cannot save
Doing good and deeds earthly done
What he failed to do, yet was required of him,
Was to trust in God's only Son.

The way that men say that will lead them to God
Is devised by Satan to obscure
He'd have man believe he is good enough
And blind him to God's only cure.

Salvation is only through God's precious blood
Accepting the Savior by faith
Not by our works, lest any might boast
This, what the scripture sayeth.

This gift of God offered freely to man
Is by grace in His mercy to all
Repenting of sin, a new life can begin
If you come when the Spirit call.

All the ways of man are of sin and death
Our sin from our God built a wall
Reconciled are we, if we bow on our knee
And prostrate at the cross choose to fall.

HOPE

While reading in Romans 15:4 the phrase "through patience and comfort of the scriptures might have hope" stands out as the source of Hope. Without hope, we are a sad and downcast lot. Yet God provides abundant hope if we want it.

As a physician board certified in emergency medicine, I see depression and the effects of depression on a daily basis in the lives and demeanor of my patients. Modern medicine's answer in treating depression with sedatives and anti-depressants is highly suspect at most and too frequently ineffective at the least. Please do not misunderstand me—there are many successes with medication and counseling, which provide insight into behavior and root causes. I am not fully discounting modern psychiatry in extreme cases. Yet

I believe for the Christian there is a better way. First Thessalonians 4:13 reveals the cause of depression as a loss of hope. In verse 18, the writer, Paul, says that having hope is a comfort to people. In Romans 15:4, Paul says that our hope comes from the scripture. Here's the problem, however: people think that by just reading the scriptures they will become a magical and holy Christian. God never promised to bless Bible readers. He blesses Bible meditators!

True hope is found in the reading of the Word of God, the meditating on it, the application of it to my life, and a relationship with Jesus Christ involving submission and confession of sin. This is hope!

(January 3, 2016)

Hope

The abundant mercy of my Lord
Gives me a life of hope
No longer must I live in fear
No more in darkness grope.

No more o'erwhelmed by circumstance
Or in sadness ways to mope
He gives me tools to firmly stand
On life's most slippery slope.

Through patience and comfort
Within the scriptures see
His desire is to fashion us
That more like Christ we'd be.

In my time of trouble sore
He is my only plea
To stand unmoved as waters rage
Like a watered tree.

Now hope I have to steady walk
Through the dark of night,
For the scripture giveth me
More abundant light.

He, my blindness gently turns
To see eternal light
The broken pieces of my life
He molds to His delight.

Do not trust in thine own self
Or in your works to save;
These will doubtless blindly end
In a Christ-less grave.

But trust thou in the grace of God
His Son, my Savior, Friend,
You'll rejoice in endless hope
And darkened paths will end.

Embrace, then, hope that God will give
And humble, you, your heart,
Then God will grant a mind of peace
And joy and hope impart

PSALM 33

As part of my daily Bible reading, I typically follow a pattern of passages in both the Old Testament and the New Testament. As dessert, I read a chapter of Psalms and a chapter of Proverbs daily. As I came across this particular psalm (33), the Lord allowed me to see it in a different way than ever before.

Verse 20 was the key verse to me; as I read it, the words just sprang into proper meter for a poem and became my opening line. I confess to changing the words "our" to "my" because it was more personal that way. Each stanza is from a different verse and together they exalt the Lord.

(January 11, 2016)

Psalm 33

My soul awaiteth for the Lord;
He is my help and shield.
My heart rejoiceth in His might,
And at His feet I yield.

His eye is on all them on Earth
The wise, His fear embrace
His mercy is their only hope
Their refuge, promised grace.

By His own words the heav'ns were made
All stand in awe of Him
For this He spake and it was done
His glories never dim.

He came to seek and save the lost
As sheep we've gone astray;
In darkness stumbling for the path
His Word alights the way.

Rejoice then in the Lord our God
Trust in His Holy Name.
Though wicked men we stand in faith
His righteousness our claim.

ONE THING IS NEEDFUL

It is not often that God gives me a poem and a tune together. I can think of only two or three times where this occurred. This poem was one of those times.

It was Sunday morning, January 17, 2016. My pastor had preached from Luke 10:38–42, the familiar story of Mary and Martha. That afternoon I pondered the words of Christ, "But one thing is needful…" Yet He doesn't exactly name that one thing. Martha's "one missing thing" was to cease from busy labor and spend time at Christ's feet.

Many Christians live at a frenetic pace. Sadly, many churches subscribe to the same philosophy of "keeping our people busy" (especially teenagers). In developing a culture in church of "busyness," we subtly insinuate that the Christian life is about "doing." The more we do and serve, the godlier we are… yet we see homes destroyed, children lost as prodigals, and churches failing. We see Christians exhausted and upset, just like Martha. The one needful thing is the development of a passionate relationship with Jesus Christ. It is to sit at His feet, as Mary was doing, and just listen.

Empty your hands, clear your calendar, pause from your hectic pace. Christ calls you to come. Sit with Him awhile. It's needful in your life.

(January 17, 2016)

One Thing Is Needful

One thing is needful,
One thing you need,
One thing you still must do,
If His Word you'll heed.

Cumbered with labor,
Work must get done.
Wrong, though, to place the task
Before time with God's Son.

Chorus:
One thing is needful
Ere your God you meet
More needful than labor:
To sit at Jesus's feet.

Bow down before His throne
Give Him your care,
Spend time with Him alone,
Meet with Him there.

Anxious and troubled
Weighed down by care
Cumbered with labor
More than you can bear.

One thing is needful
Ere labor you start
Bow at the Savior's feet,
And give Him your heart.

Chorus

Impatient before the Lord
Demanding He act
Trying to force His hand
His wisdom you lacked.

Defining how God must move
We tell Him what to do
Forgetting His way is just
His plan is best for you.

MY HYMN OF JOY

As the music minister in my church, I often tease the congregation when we sing certain hymns by saying "this hymn is number 4 (or another number) in the top ten hymns list." I have developed a list of my top ten hymns—songs that I dearly love because of the words, the passage of scripture they are taken from or a memory they evoke. Music is such a powerful communication tool.

When our church has a baptismal service, as the pastor prepares himself, I allow the congregation to request "favorites". While some ornery children view this time as an opportunity to "stump the song leader," others select thoughtful songs with deep meaning. It was following one of these baptismal services that I pondered the list of my top ten hymns and was able to write a song including all of the titles. This was a really fun poem to write!

(January 17, 2016)

Photo Credit: Vonda Murdock

My Hymn of Joy

To leave this body in the twinkling of an eye
To be present forever with my King
His blood in mercy He so freely gave
In heaven forever will I sing.

"II WILL BE WORTH IT ALL" is one that I'll surely shout
Eternally grateful, His blood has washed my sins all out
"GREAT IS THY FAITHFULNESS" I'll see at last first hand
As I view forever Canaan's land.

"A CHILD OF THE KING" I'll sing in joyful praise
With my "HAVEN OF REST" I'll spend eternal days
"ABIDE WITH ME" no need I'll have to ask
"FACE TO FACE," no veil His beauty there will mask.

"IT IS WELL" my soul there surely knows
In peace, to walk with Sharon's Rose
"THE UNVEILED CHRIST" I'll call my Friend
And "DAY BY DAY" will never end.

No need to pray as on Earth when skies were brass
Once through this fervent I shall forever pass
"SWEET HOUR OF PRAYER" I'll cast aside.
For with my Savior I'll then abide.

LAMENT OF AMOS

While reading in the book of Amos, I came across the "Lament of Amos" in chapter 2. This chapter is a grieving call of judgment on Judah and Israel. Especially poignant is verse 13, where God describes Himself pressed down by the sin of people as a "cart is pressed that is full of sheaves." It was grieving because God had chastised His people over and over but they did not recognize their troubles were brought on by their sin, or if they did, they were unconcerned.

Either way, it is a woeful lament of a man pleading for God's people to get right with Him... and they would not hear him.

(January 27, 2016)

Lament of Amos

As a cart is pressed, which is full of sheaves
So we weigh down our God,
Set Him aside and despise His Word,
Make the gulf between us broad.

We turn aside all the ways of the meek
And drink the wine of the lost,
Turning our back on the mercy of God.
We get wealth at any cost.

What will we do when He kindles a fire
To burn our dross away?
Will we even see it's the hand of God
That visits us that day?

What does it take for a heart to repent
A heart once knit to God?
Wise is the man who will turn at His call
And not require the rod.

VISIONS OF ZECHARIAH

This poem is a different type of poem. It was written while on a cruise (see back story to the "Potter's Field"), and I had many hours of leisure in which to research, study, and attempt to understand an otherwise difficult passage of scripture, the Visions of Zechariah seen in Zechariah 1:7 through 6:15.

I must say, however, this was a very fun poem to write because I had to first understand each vision and then distill it to a simple few sentences. After I completed it, I shared the poem with my wife and daughters at dinner (they were on the cruise with me). It was very obvious they were, well, underwhelmed. I think I could read on their faces the question they dared not ask, "Has Dad gone crazy?"

Nonetheless, this is a good chronicle of the ten visions of Zechariah... at least I like it!

(January 31, 2016)

Visions of Zechariah

In visions Zechariah showed
Though countless years passed by
That God's not laid His love aside
For the apple of His eye.

Israel will exalted be
Above all on the Earth
Through them are blessings from God's hand
Like a humble Savior's birth.

First he saw a vision clear
Of Christ on speckled horse
Who stood within the myrtle grove
Observing Israel's course.

When Christ first came as carpenter
(Still man His message spurns)
Yet Zechariah says in chapter one
This carpenter returns.

Exacting judgment on the horns
Of Gentile powers once grand
Who dared to rise against the Lord
To move Israel from their land.

Fourth he saw a measuring line
His city to rebuild
He, a wall of fire without
Within, His glory filled.

Next he saw unrighteous man
In rags in his own might,
Accused by Satan at God's throne
Then robed in garments white.

Redeemed by Christ, by mercy's blood
No other cause to plea;
One day the blinders will be off
This nation then will see.

The Branch, the Servant of the Lord,
This man though humble be,
Wounded in the house of friends
Messiah now they see.

Then candlestick and olive trees
A headstone crying, "Grace!"
Not by power or by man's might
His Spirit we embrace.
The scroll which flyeth over all,
Accusing man of sin;
By it unrighteousness is judged
Against both God and man.

An ephah women held aloft
Burdened down with lead
The church's greed in Babylon
"Wicked!" the angel said.

Lastly, chariots numbering four
Render judgment on the Earth
Prepare the way for Priestly King
He of infinite worth.

A STRUGGLE WITH GOD

In reading Zechariah 7:11–14, there is the phrase "an adamant stone." This is an interesting word, especially in light of verse 11, which describes the willful rebellious heart. It not only refuses to hearken but also pulls away the shoulder in overt rejection. Then comes the next verse "yea, they made their hearts as an adamant stone."

At 4:00 a.m., God awoke me with that phrase. I got up from my bed on the cruise ship (see back story for "The Potter's Field") and sat at the desk to reread that chapter. God broke my heart as I caught a glimpse of Zechariah's broken heart, pleading for people to repent and submit to God yet they have set their heart as an adamant stone. How God's heart aches when His children turn away from Him!

God, give me a heart soft to your truth, ears eager to hear your still, small voice, and a shoulder desirous to nestle in your bosom.

(February 5, 2016)

A Struggle with God

Have I made my heart an adamant stone,
Which turns from the Word of God?
Do I pull away and stop my ears?
Am I deaf as the earthen sod?

When God cries out and I will not hear,
He has promised the same unto me,
As my troubles mount and I need a way out,
His deliverance I will not see.

Do I harden my heart as the Word is preached?
When God calls do I hesitate?
If I do, He has said this my just reward:
He will make my life desolate.

As a desert in the heat when the sun beats down
So my life will be dry as well
No joy in my heart as I daily walk
My life just an empty shell.

If I gather friends who know not the Lord
From His way I'll be further led,
I will say to my heart "my own way I will chart"
And the path will be hard that I tread.

An adamant heart God can never use
A willful heart of stone.
To refuse to submit, in His face you spit
Though the truth you've been often shown.

Yet God offers me hope if I yield Him my heart,
Surrender my feeble fight,
Give Him my life and resist Him no more,
Confess that His way is right.

THE POTTER'S FIELD

While on a cruise to the Caribbean in January 2016, my Bible reading took me to Zechariah. I had a glorious time in the scripture and found myself able to spend many hours each day in reading and contemplating the passages. In Zechariah 11:12–14, we find the prophecy of the betrayal of Jesus Christ and the silver given Judas being used to purchase a potter's field. This sent my mind back to Jeremiah 18:1–6 and Matthew 26 and 27, also in reference to the potter.

The price of the Lord of the universe in the eyes of wicked man was a mere thirty pieces of silver. Because it was the price of blood, the high priest was not able to return the money to the treasury. To think that all that money could buy was a useless plot of ground is sobering. Yet when we consider that the Master Potter's heart is to restore useless and broken things, it is a beautiful tribute. His delight is to heal our hurts and repair us, the broken.

In this poem, I wanted to convey a lack of patience on the part of the earthly potter and a finality to his cast-off works. Yet it is the precious blood of Christ that actually paid for that piece of land and it gave Him the right to work in the potter's field!

(February 6, 2016)

The Potter's Field

The potter's field, a desolate place
Where the potter threw the clay,
Which would not yield to his control,
And there forever it lay.

How oft' the earthly potter tried
When the clay was in his hand
To mold it to a useful thing
To conform to his demand.

But if the clay would not submit
He'd remove it from his wheel
And break in two that lump of clay
It's flaws he'd not conceal.

So in the potter's field there lay
Clay void of any worth
Broken pieces unaware
Of a Master Potter's birth.

This Potter grew into humble man
Without sin or flaw
Yet sold for silver by a friend
Then smote they on his jaw.

In haste, the High Priest bought the plot,
The worthless potter's field,
Wherein lay the broken clay
The ones that would not yield.

Then with His blood Christ bought that field
Redeemed it for His own
And gleaned there in the useless plot
Where the broken clay was thrown.

He gathered pieces cast aside
Rejected by all men,
With wounded hands then placed them on
The potter's wheel again.

For each piece He had a plan
The will of God above
In mercy fashioned each into
A vessel of His love.

MY PRAISE

The subtle sin of pride has so many faces, and I have written several poems on this subject. Even in our "praises to God," it can rear its evil head. Satan slyly blinds Christians to the wickedness in our own hearts—"The heart is deceitful above all things, and desperately wicked, who can know it?" (Jeremiah 17:9)—and sometimes as we stand to give God praise we want to make sure everyone acknowledges how great we think we are as well. So our "praises" sometimes can be a subtle way to steal God's glory. Hannah, in 1 Samuel 2:3, noticed this pride in the testimony and prayers of others. She cautioned against it in her prophetic prayer in this passage.

Apart from the Word of God revealing these blind spots in our lives, we go on sinning in blissful ignorance yet dishonoring God. In fact, the very next verse in Jeremiah 17:10 says that God searches and knows the hearts of every man. The only way we can know what's in our heart is by asking God in our quiet time. If we are not diligent in this area, we commit sins that to our eyes are "secret" (Psalm 19:12; 90:8), but secret only to us.

This poem's title was intended to reflect the thought not of praise for God, but praise for me: "My Praise."

(February 26, 2016)

My Praise

I stand to give a praise to God,
A testimony sure,
Let me boast on this thing first
My heart, that's oh so pure.

Men daily speak so well of me
God must be very proud
I stand to tell my friends I'm swell
I give Him praise so loud.

I'm grateful that I do His work
And that others see me there
Follow, ye, my example, too
"Be holy, like me" my prayer.

I stand to give my praise to God
As we prepare to pray
You mean I can't exalt myself?
… never mind, I have nothing to say.

YOUR HOUSE

Psalm 84 speaks eloquently of the love a person can have for the House of God. In the Old Testament, this yearning to be at the temple was likely more intense because the Holy Spirit did not indwell a person then (this occurred in the New Testament in Acts 2). The closeness to God was experienced when man obeyed the commandments of God and worshipped as prescribed in the law. This obedience was counted as faith, according to Hebrews 11.

In the church age, where we are now in history, the Holy Spirit indwells a believer at the moment of salvation and guides them into truth as he submits to Him. That relationship with God matures, strengthens, encourages, and refreshes, bringing peace into his life as a believer.

Sadly, so many Christians live a dry, thirsty life because they never have a close relationship with God. They come to Him only in times of crisis or trouble, treating Him as a "good luck charm" and not the God of the universe. Since there is no such named place in Israel, the Valley of Baca mentioned in this psalm is considered an allegory for the place of sorrow or suffering in a person's life—a dry place.

This psalm speaks of the yearning in a man's spirit for the presence of God. While Satan would have us fill this void with things of the world which can never satisfy (drugs, alcohol, illicit relationships, pleasure lifestyle), only God will satisfy the thirst in a man's soul.

(February 28, 2016, from Psalm 84)

Your House

From strength to strength
God calls we grow
To walk in the Spirit
The Savior to know.

In the Valley of Baca
You make there a well
Though sorrow encompass
And troubles assail.

The rain filleth pools
In the land of my fathers
But there will You lead
Beside living waters.

Whence cometh this strength
To a dry thirsty man?
To empower him labor
As the younger men can?

To dwell in the House
Of my Savior and Lord
He strengthens, equips
With His shield and His sword.

His presence provides
New strength every day
You'll withhold not a thing
As I bow down to pray.

Your House, Lord, I love
So my heart crieth out
My spirit's refreshed
Thus endeth my drought.

UNWORTHY

I started this poem when I started "A Trophy of Grace" in July 2015. I was simply overwhelmed by the mercy of God who provided an outstretched hand to wicked man. And when I say "wicked man," I mean, specifically, me. I truly stand amazed at the compassionate Christ who had nothing to gain by His painful sacrifice, yet He suffered at the hands of His own creation. The poem (and song) "My Jesus Fair" written by Chris Anderson well speaks of the irony that He who made the thorns was later pierced by them; He who knew no sin became sin for me and was judged by God while I was set free! I wonder at the sacrifice of perfect God at the hands of flawed man (Romans 5:8).

I weep when I consider so great the sacrifice of my pure Savior and how, in the person of Holy God, this was the only sacrifice acceptable to Himself (Isaiah 53:10–11, John 4:10). Unworthy I am… and worthy He is.

(March 2, 2016)

Unworthy

Insufficient, Unworthy
The chiefest of sinners I am
Undeserving the least of His mercy and love
Yet for me shed the blood of the Lamb.

So unworthy this sinner
To be viewed with merciful eyes.
In pity He saw me, in love drew me close,
The cords of my bondage unties.

Unworthy the cry
Of the hopeless unlovely outcast;
Unaware there is hope in the fountain of love
To erase the shame of my past.

Yes, unworthy the sinner
In anguish, whose rags are his best
Who falls at the feet of the Source of all hope
Who doubtless will find there his rest.

Ashamed and unworthy
Undeserving, I know that I am
Yet forgiven I bow at the foot of His cross
And find mercy at the feet of the Lamb.

RESTORED SIGHT

The imagery in Zechariah 13 is simply beautiful. It begins by describing how a fountain of mercy has been opened to the nation of Israel in their most trying hour. All the world has come against them by the close of the Great Tribulation. They have no hope except for the salvation of the Lord.

Christ, as the true shepherd of Israel, presents Himself to His people in direct contrast to the false shepherd mentioned in Zechariah 11:15–17. Israel examines Him, asking about the wounds in His hands. His reply in verse six is heart breaking. They realize who He is and repent as a nation and, as a result, see the mighty salvation of the Lord. This ushers in the Millennial Kingdom and is the fulfillment of His promise of rest offered them during His first advent.

The Bible speaks of the blindness of Israel (2 Corinthians 3:14–15; Romans 11:7–36) and its purpose to provoke Israel to jealousy (Romans 11:11). While the road of persecution Israel has had to walk saddens me, I am grateful that their blindness permitted the grafting in of the Gentile branch! Do not be confused, gentle reader; the apple of god's eye is Israel and they will be restored to their rightful place at God's side and will rule all nations for one thousand years!

(March 3, 2016)

Restored Sight

A fountain of cleansing, hope for man's sin
In the Day of the Lord opened wide
Wounds suffered He in the house of His friends
Make them see how their Savior had died.

Rejected was He, man of sorrows and shame
When He came first to offer them rest
As a lamb to the slaughter, He spake not a word
As their King, to them NOW manifest.

O, what sorrow they'll feel, on their knees they will kneel
When they see what they've done to their Lord
"My God and my King," raising hands they will sing
Now on them will His grace be outpoured.

Once jealous of His work among heathen
Once bitter for the path they have trod
The Spirit of God removes blinders
And the Jews shout, "The Lord is my God!"

Photo Credit: Public Domain

163

KINSMAN REDEEMER

In my devotions today, I was reading in Ruth. My practice is to accompany my Bible reading with the reading of a commentary paralleling the passage (each year as I read my Bible through, I change the commentary I use so I get multiple perspectives on Bible passages). During this particular reading, I was using J. Vernon McGee's commentary and found this phrase concerning Ruth: "She found grace in the eyes of the Kinsman Redeemer." That sentence impacted me and I considered the qualities of the Kinsman Redeemer that caused him to reach out in love and mercy and compassion to an outcast. And she was an outcast. Naomi had even warned her that if she accompanied her back to Bethlehem-Judah, she would not be able to marry because she was a Moabite and the Jews held them in low regard.

Knowing this, Ruth nonetheless embraced Naomi's God and returned with her to her ancestral home. The redemption of God is so beautifully displayed in this small book. God redeemed us, not once, but twice. Our life is His because He created us and gave us life—yet, He also bought us back from sin, much like Hosea bought his wife a second time. God, as our Kinsman Redeemer, had the first legal right to redeem us out of sin's hold—praise His name that He did not pass on that right!

(March 4, 2016)

Kinsman Redeemer

As Godly sorrow worketh repentance,
Ruth committed to follow the Lord
Turning her back on her homeland
The gods of Moab deplored.

"Whither thou goest I go also"
Was her pledge to her mother in law.
"The Hope of your people is my Hope
I'll draw from the well that you draw."

Boaz with compassion looked on her
Though an outcast, a Moabite, she
He lifted her eyes to behold him
When for refuge to him she did flee.

Grace in the eyes of the Kinsman
When no reason for mercy is found
No reason to lift one so broken
But love in his heart did abound.

Her decision to follow Naomi
And to Jehovah always to cling
Results in her lineage King David
And Christ, our Savior and King.

The Lord is our Kinsman Redeemer
Who redeemed us with His precious blood
No beauty in us that would move Him
To love in His unending flood.

II

Poems on Family and Home

THE EMPTY ROOM

When Gina, my firstborn child, was four years old, I wrote this poem. I had wanted a more active role in my daughter's childhood than I saw in the generations preceding ours, so it became my "job" early on to be the playtime ringleader and the bedtime snuggler.

Within seconds of coming home from work, our playtime began. As she grew older, it changed from "toys on the floor" to backyard play to local park play. At bedtime, we had a set ritual—as a small child, I would sing her to seep in my lap—"K-K-K-Katy, Cici My Playmate, Hush Little Baby, and Danny Boy" always had to be included! I would finish and would say, "Just one more song."

Her reply was "No, three!" We held these negotiations night after night for many years. Belly rubs, back rubs, kissing like a fish were usually required. When she got older and lanky (and laps shrunk), she would crawl under her covers and I had to lay on top the covers beside her and sing a few more songs.

I'm not sure exactly when it all changed, but as she matured and became more independent, she no longer needed these rituals and that is understandable. But frankly, I think I needed them more than her... and I sure miss them.

(July 16, 1985, fourth birthday of my daughter, Gina)

The Empty Room

In my mind in several years
I'll sit beside my wife,
And listen to my daughter's voice
The echoes of my life.
Her cries of "Daddy, watch me"
And calls of "Mommy, look!"
And tender eyes just begging
To read her one more book.
She loves to hear her Daddy sing,
"Just one more song!"
"No three!"
And tender eyes are pleading
"Daddy, lay beside of me."
"And scratch my belly and rub my back."
And "Kiss me like a fish."
Oh, if I could choose the Master's plan,
This would be my wish:
That time would stop, the moments halt,
She'd feel no sorrow nor pain;
Within her days that God would give
Her blessings like the rain.

But time won't stop and pain will come
And heartache she will feel;
And this is why her Mom and Dad
With humbled hearts would kneel.
To seek His face and ask His will
To break our hearts asunder;
To look upon our daughter's face
And marvel at His wonder.
Behind those eyes, a caring heart,
So like her Mom, my wife;
I'll look upon these moments now,
… The echoes of my life.
As years pass on, a voice I hear,
Growing fainter, for ears fade, you see;
Calling gently on the wind,
"Daddy, won't you play with me?"
Though her room is vacant now,
I'll turn off her bedroom light;
And close the door so softly,
To my child's room each night.

IT WAS YOU

As I drove alone from South Carolina to Georgia where Rachel was visiting her mother, my thoughts turned to my precious wife and her influence on my life. It was our fifth wedding anniversary. Seven years before, I was a new Christian and had experienced little growth. Additionally, I had a glaring character flaw: a real issue with anger. While I had tried to keep this hidden, Rachel saw through my facade and suggested we study the Bible together. We started reading the Bible and friends suggested additional Christian books that we devoured. This helped to lay a great foundation for our marriage later.

This poem was written during a major decision period in my life. Having returned from Saudi Arabia only two months prior, I wrestled with the decision of leaving the air force and going to medical school. The trilogy of poems, "The Journey," "The Lighthouse," and "The Champion," reflect this struggle. This poem also highlights that struggle as well. Much of what I am today in regards to the successes in my life are a direct result of the encouragement I have received from my wife.

One caveat on this poem: the entire last stanza is in quotations because I plagiarized it from a song I heard on this drive from South Carolina. I do not recall the song or artist, so it is not credited.

(August 15, 1985, dedicated to my wife Rachel on our fifth wedding anniversary)

It Was You

I hear people say that I've got it made,
But my struggles they seldom can see;
If they only knew just how much of you,
Went into the making of me.

When the poem in my heart was a whisper,
And the melody seemed so wrong;
It was you who gave me the vision,
And inspired in me a new song.

When all hope was hidden within me,
And my dreams just seemed so far;
It was you who gave me the courage,
And convinced me to follow my star.

When discouragement hit me hardest,
And of my goals I'd lost the sight;
By you I was gently encouraged
To stand fast and continue to fight.

I was a young bird lying injured,
Who had lost the desire to sing;
Now I'll soar as high as an eagle
For you've healed my broken wing.

"I'm a captain within his vessel,
out upon the storm-tossed sea;
but the only thing I require,
is my lady alongside of me."

BABY VALENTINE

I wrote this poem when Gina was only several months old (1981). I imagined what it would be like raising a girl and watching her mature into a young lady. This poem remained unfinished until four years later when I added the last stanza.

With the four years difference from the body of the poem and the last stanza, a distinct change of perspective is perceived. In the final stanza and with the passage of time, I came to the realization that I needed to enjoy the moments—the "nows" in her life—because tomorrow will come soon enough.

Why "Baby Valentine"? This was one name I called Gina as an infant. She was also called Sputnik, Gina-Bug, Punkin', Scooter, and a *host* of others!

(November 4, 1985)

Baby Valentine

With my daughter's hand in mine,
She's my sweet baby valentine;
And I carry her to the park,
We stay out till long after dark.

With my daughter's hand I mine,
We stand in the skating rink line;
And we skate around and whirl,
For she's my Valentine girl.

With my daughter's hand in mine,
I realize that all is fine;
But I see that she's growing so fast,
And our time, so fleeting, won't last.

With my daughter's hand in mine,
I'll walk with her one last time;
I'll cover my tears with a smile,
As I walk her down the aisle.

And I'll be left with just my dreams,
Of her aches, her pains, her teens;
And I'll smile with tears on my face,
For another man's taking my place.

She's my sweet Baby Valentine,
And for now she's only mine,
And each night I'll kiss her cheek,
Then go to my own room and weep;.
For my sweet Baby Valentine,
Will too soon, no longer be mine.

MY BROTHER, MY FRIEND

It is true that no man stands alone. The self-made man is a myth, for everyone has help in one fashion or another. This is true in my life as well. Down through the years, I have had help from each of my siblings, my parents, and Rachel's parents. One person stands out, however, above the rest. My brother, Dave, has been an incredible source of encouragement to me. He has the most giving heart of any man I know.

When the Bible speaks of the spiritual gift of giving, we are shortsighted when we only interpret that in financial terms, and I think that is true with David as well. He is a selfless man who sacrifices his time and counsel to help others. When he became a Christian, he reached out to others and was instrumental in my eldest brother's conversion (Mike) to Christ.

As a young man, when I did stupid things, he was the one who bailed me out (sorry about the car, Mom). When I was in medical school, he often gave food and money to help my family survive.

I wrote this poem as I was about to graduate premed at the University of South Carolina as a tribute to him for the help he had given me in the past.

David, I will forever be indebted to you. Thank you.

(March 13, 1990, dedicated to my brother David Veach)

My Brother, My Friend

In the days of our youth
(these many years past)
I wish I had taken the time
To stop the race; to slow the pace,
And talk with you brother mine.

To learn of your goals, your dreams, your plans
To share the inner thought;
To glean of the wisdom you possess,
To act as a brother ought.

But I've wasted the time that should have been spent
In getting to know you better.
Your compassionate heart, so freely you give
And I find, once again, I'm a debtor.

As we wax older and time precious grows,
My ways you'll see shall amend;
For I've seen in you, compassion true
… and you're not just a brother, but friend.

THE BUILDER

Jonathan's poem came very quickly. First of all, it should be said that as a handyman, I am a complete and utter failure! I once built a doghouse that leaned so much the dog refused to enter it, choosing instead to sit beside it in the pouring rain. My solution was to place it next to a telephone pole in our backyard and nail it to the pole. She still wouldn't go inside!

So my tools are (were) pretty pristine as they saw little actual use. Nonetheless, every minor project (pounding a nail, hanging a picture and such) involved a process whereby my entire toolbox was brought into the house and "Tool Boy" pulled *every* tool out. Rarely, however, did they make their way back. None of my tools ever broke from overuse, but countless hundreds died a lonely, rusty death in the yard....

(April 28, 1995, Jonathan's fourth birthday)

The Builder

I've projects that number a thousand,
Many things I've meant to do;
Repairs undone in the household,
Though I've tried a time or two.

But each time a job is selected
Comes a helper to my side:
It's "Tool Boy" to the rescue,
With a grin a mile wide.

His joyful chatter makes me chuckle
But the jobs never quite get done:
For my tools all seem to scatter,
As he examines them one by one.

A hammer I found 'neath his pillow
And a wrench behind his door
A saw beneath his dresser
And my drill inside his drawer.

And so we work this way for minutes
Till our job gives way to play
And repairs once again are postponed
To be completed another day.

As my work again sits unfinished
Frustration from joy starts to press
I'd be quicker without his assistance
To build *alone* I feel would be best.

I could finish the task so much faster
Unhindered is best, I surmise
Then my thoughts turn to projects ongoing
And taking stock of my goal realize:

That of all the projects I've started
Countless many I've left undone
This one I return to with pleasure:
With love, I am building a son.

SONGBIRD

Few children loved music like Laura. As a small child, she sang all the time. Literally… as soon as her feet hit the floor she was singing and continued throughout the day. Often, when we needed to find her in the home we only had to listen for her song. A favorite activity of hers (and mine) was for her to crawl into my lap and sing her repertoire while I quietly sat (and yes, sometimes dozed).

I also called Laura my "Butterfly Princess" because she never met a stranger. She was always so confident of herself and so independent minded that she could talk to anyone—and would!

This poem was written rather easily, but the final stanza brought tears to my own eyes as I considered, "What might it take for me to no longer hear Laura's song?" Her song is so special to me that the possible answers to that question drove me to my knees to pray for not only her but also each of my children. For their safety, their hearts, their relationship with God, and their futures. Sing on, precious Songbird.

(Written for Laura, April 26, 2002)

Songbird

"I love you, Daddy, from here to here,"
She'd say with arms spread wide
Her face a mere reflection
Of the joy she holds inside.

Her mischievous smile, her impish grin
Would melt the coldest heart
And so she'd crawl into my lap
Her music soon to start.

"Who wants to hear me sing a song?"
She'd ask of anyone near;
Though some protest (I must confess)
She'd sing for all to hear.

She would gesture and dance about my feet
And I'd stumble to my chair
My "Butterfly Princess" she could be
Flitting tirelessly everywhere.

On trips we would take her voice I'd hear
Above the noise of others.
She'd sing her list from top to bottom
One right after another.

But now I gaze as the sun slowly sets
The shadows of my life growing long
Content I'd be, in silence sit
To listen, again, to her song.

RACHEL'S EYES

Nearly four decades ago, I first saw her eyes. It was June 1978, and she was singing a duet in church (Bible Baptist Temple, Warner Robins, GA). I don't remember the song, but I have never forgotten the eyes. Quite frankly, I was mesmerized. Many people refute the possibility of love at first sight but I fell for her that day and it was her eyes that drew me in. To this day when I am in a crowded room, I look for her eyes to catch mine.

This poem was written after a prolonged trip to Italy in January 2012. As I pondered the beauty of Italy, her eyes were still more beautiful to me. The classical women of beauty which inspired desire in men, Helen of Troy, Juliet and Venus, the objects of beauty that move men to action—the beauty of Venice, Rome, and Pisa—do not compare to her. And now, nearly four decades after glimpsing those eyes—they still draw me in!

(April 3, 2012)

Rachel's Eyes

These eyes that drew me these many years past,
These eyes, when on me, my heart flutters fast.
When across the room, I search for their gaze,
No love ere could fathom, as I count out the ways.

Even she, whose face, caused ships' sails to raise,
Nor her, the Venus, whose beauty men praise.
Poe's Helen, so precious, Will's Juliet, though rare,
Not of these beauties, to her could compare.

Not waters of Venice, nor ruins of Rome,
Not breathtaking grandeur of a vast Florence dome.
Though to each of these splendors, men attribute Rome's rise,
All are found wanting when compared to her eyes.

Green and so gentle, on mercy she took,
Forgiving shortcomings, reassure with a look.
The depth of their beauty, within me inspire,
Devotion everlasting, and a fiery desire.

Worlds searched for this passion, most men ne'er realize
For me is found truly, in the depths of her eyes.

EVENING

My wife and I have a great relationship. She has always been my best friend and the one with whom I would spend every waking moment if it were possible. One blessing of my heart surgery in September 2012 was that I got to spend nearly six unbroken weeks with her. That may seem difficult to many couples but my wife and I crave each others' company, and we never tire of one another.

It was in the weeks following my heart surgery that I wrote this poem. She had encouraged me to sit with her one evening as the sun set. As we sat together, hand in hand, I retraced the years of our lives. This was what I wanted when we married thirty-two (at the time) years ago. I wanted to grow old together with her.

I thought of some of the things which seemed so difficult early in our marriage (boulders then), were inconsequential now (pebbles). While we have always had a great relationship, God had allowed our love to mature and we were at peace as we sat together. How comfortable I am with my precious wife and how I treasure her company. Rachel, my love, I will always love you and I am grateful to God for borrowed time.

(October 13, 2012)

Evening

Autumn air around us crisp
Daylight nearly done
Beside her now, we stand and gaze
On the setting sun.

Evening slowly settles in,
And with it labor's rest
Daytime struggles vivid once,
Now fade to nothingness.

Though pebbles mark the trail we walk,
T'was a stony path before,
Once hurried then is now a walk,
Of two along a shore.

Hand in hand with fingers laced
At ease I must confess,
Treasure found, sought so long:
Comfort in Love's caress.

Photo Credit: Rachel Veach

JOURNEY'S END

My career as an emergency physician had evolved steadily down through the years. I became an ER medical director in 1999, and within several years, had oversight of eight, then twenty-seven, and eventually sixty-four ERs. With this position came travel—a lot of it! As I drove from one ER to another, I wrote a lot of poems in my mind but few committed to paper. Although in my current position I have a much more reasonable oversight of fewer ERs, I still travel countless miles.

This poem was intended to represent my longing to be home with my family. As the words came, however, this desire to go home became a euphemism for my earthly walk and my desire to go to heaven. The comfort I speak of is the embrace of my precious wife and family. The deeper meaning, however, is as I've matured in the Lord, the things that *once* rattled me now hold no power over me. As I have learned submission to Him, He has quieted my soul.

(June 8, 2013)

Journey's End

This road that carries me now far away
Will bring me again homeward one day;
Endless miles alone and lost in deep thought
Reflecting on paths taken, and ones taken not.

As evening falls quickly the sun lags behind
Endless journey as roads before me unwind
Scenery passing astoundingly fast
Making my way home to rest now at last.

Loving voices sound the beacon towards home
But miles to go ere rest sweeter be won
Home's soon arrival to bask in the light
Evening sun settles into quiet of night.

This road travelled less (or not, I can't say)
Others may judge at the close of my day
This one thing I know and eager will lend
That comfort I found at my journey's end.

OF BUGS AND SUCH

I had a blast writing Jessica's poem. As I pondered her personality and deeds (misdeeds?) I could only laugh. At sixteen, she came running into the house holding a frog in her hands. Out of its mouth protruded a half eaten worm. Needless to say, Mom, well… sort of freaked. I laughed and told her to take it outside. She did, but not before watching the frog eat the rest of the worm. Ugh…

Jessica is very subtle with her expressions of love. Like watching the ocean waters for a majestic whale to surface, Jessica's hugs and kisses come suddenly and unexpectedly and all I can do is enjoy the moment.

(October 17, 2013, for Jessica)

Of Bugs and Such

Of frogs and bugs and things disgust
Of turtles and other stuff messy
These best describe the spirit of
My youngest daughter Jessie.

When as an infant her eyes were turned
To animals, four legged and more
And, oh what a sight, her mother affright
When outside was brought indoor.

Turtles in boxes, frogs housed in cans
"Watch them closely" her parents implored
Alas, I confess, to her mother's distress
Their containment was rarely secured.

A compassionate friend to four-legged kind
To cats and dogs and animals such
These things important, her heart was so drawn
But to order? Well, not so much.

Her heart so tender, to things godly drawn
A gentleness all of her own
A lady, yet tomboy, a socialite true
Yet content to sit reading alone.

Her hugs and snuggles are quietly craved
Her kisses, a treasure to hold
Her expressions of love learned from her Father above
Will warm me 'til my arms last I fold.

UNSUNG HERO

A photo of my father sits on the filing cabinet at my desk in my office. I often look at it and utter a praise to God for the life of my father.

He was, to my mind, an enigma. He was a hard man to get to know through a child's "drive by" contacts. As a small child, I tried to avoid him as contact usually resulted in the assigning of chores! As I grew older, I learned to enter his space, the darkened living room where he sat on the couch, and just sit with him, not speaking. Eventually he would speak, when he saw that I was going to remain there. The discussions we had in that darkened room were the great lessons of my life. He told me about honest labor, about responsibility, and even about investing (okay, those talks I never understood. To this day, I don't know a thing about "puts" and "shorts" when playing the stock market!).

When he died in 1999, I felt a hole had been torn out of my heart. At his death, he was not considered a "great man" by the world. He was not considered a learned man yet he did math equations for fun. He had a mild speech impediment yet his silence spoke more volumes than most of man's speeches. Yet he had six children who knew how to work hard, love their families, and all six honored God with their lives.

Dad, you were great to me and you were my hero.

(October 26, 2013)

Unsung Hero

Fading photos, the sum of a man
Reduced to a memory to some
Bent with the labor of a hard life
Weathered and worn he'd become.

What tribute is given to the man who works hard?
The man not eloquent, not artist nor bard?
Can't this man, not learned, be high in regard?
The one for his family who was ever on guard?

We elevate men for foolish things in this land
Who excel in sports, or who lead the band
Who climb up the ladder, achieve success as they planned
But celebrate him, the one who held out his hand.

A life unlauded, yet on him many fates hung
Unrecognized greatness in the eyes of the young
By the sweat of his brow, a living was wrung
For this man lived the life of the hero unsung.

NEEDING INSTRUCTION

My son, Stephen, was (as he likes to tell his siblings) the only child we chose. We fostered Stephen at the age of six and adopted him at the age of eight.

I met Stephen in the hallway of our church in Little Rock, AR, and he melted my heart. When I approached the family about fostering him, with the intent to adopt him, it was a unanimous "yes."

His funny statements and deeds down through the years have become legend. In the courthouse on adoption day he had obtained fake "bubba teeth" and wore them, smiling widely as he stood before the judge. For Christmas that first year, most of the toys were for him—and he seemed incredibly thrilled with a little set of sponges in the shape of a hammer (Bob the Builder) we had purchased at the dollar store. On a month long RV trip, he threw up as we were backing out of the driveway!

In San Antonio, we videotaped him as he ate an ice cream cone, and as the vapor ascended from the ice cream, he squealed, "My ice cream's got smoke!" He slammed every door he closed—home, car, restaurant—and he had to be taught how to close doors. Once, Jonathan got the surprise of his life as he stood on the front porch. From Stephen's second-story room came a steady stream of fluid splashing at his feet. Stephen, to keep from coming downstairs to use the bathroom, had simply cut his window screen and "let it go"— much to Jonathan's dismay! The most famous Stephen story involved a conspiracy over a glass of poured milk and... well, that's a story Laura and Stephen can tell!

(December 16, 2014)

Needing Instruction

Needing instruction, you approached me that day
While wandering in the hall
You, a boy of only five,
Me, a stranger tall.

"Mister, can you help me find my class?"
As your hand reached up to mine,
So together we walked, hand in hand,
On our quest your room to find.

Two years later before a judge we stood
You with "Bubba teeth" grin
Your mischievous smile belied the truth
Of the struggles you faced within.

Needing instruction on a number of things,
Like riding a bike and more,
From sponges and ice cream to RV trips
And how to close a door.

But instruction NOT needed on other fronts
On your own you learned these it seems,
Building allegiance over poured milk
And reasons to cut window screens.

As years passed on your personality bloomed
Your humor you'd subtly display
Needing instruction on when to say what
Our love for you grew day by day.

From boy to a man, too soon you grew
Giving instruction I thought that my chore
Looking back these years, this I have learned
That I needed instruction the more.

195

CAST IN STONE

This poem was written as a love song to my wife. It has three verses and the chorus is the second quatrain. I am crazy, madly, passionately in love with my wife and have been so since 1978! I can truly say that absence from her makes my heart ache to return. Unfortunately, my work requires a lot of travel to the emergency rooms I oversee.

En route to these hospitals my mind is focused on the agenda of things I must accomplish while on site. But once homeward bound, my thoughts inevitably turn to my family and to my precious wife in particular.

In a meeting with a hospital CEO earlier in the day on June 20, 2014, he said, "And you can cast it in stone." Although I had heard the phrase numerous times before, this day I pondered it as I drove back to Little Rock from Oklahoma.

"Cast in Stone." There are a lot of things about God of which this could be said. God's love, His mercy, His faithfulness, His loving kindness… the list is endless! But as my heart and thoughts were increasingly focused on my wife as I drew closer to home, I considered our relationship. That, too, could be described as "cast in stone." As Proverbs 31 implies, to a loving and faithful wife a memorial should be built! This poem/song was written as a memorial to my wife and because of the yearning in my heart when I am apart from her.

(December 19, 2014)

Cast in Stone

How does one measure
The love in a heart?
And how does one know
When that love got its start?

They say love at first sight
Seldom will last
But they don't see how
That love was first cast.

Cast in stone: from a pebble
A mountain has grown
Steadfast love, now together
Two hearts have been sewn.

Where once was a void
Now never alone
Where once so afraid
Now fears have all flown
CAST IN STONE.

When we are apart, and her eyes I can't see
I long for her presence, so homeward I flee
To my place of protection, her loving embrace
To the warmth of her comfort, and beautiful face.

Through a forest of darkness, a path has been shown
Through a lifetime of sharing, in her eyes I am known
Her soft easy laughter, is healing to me
To be lost in her eyes, so contented I'd be
CAST IN STONE.

A WALK

In my job as a physician, I not only work in ERs but I also oversee a number of ERs across the country as the senior vice president for an ER management company.

October 2015 saw me in the state of Washington where I managed four ERs. As I drove the long, cold, nearly desolate highway between Spokane and Seattle (as often occurs when I am away from my precious wife), my thoughts turned to Rachel and my immense love for her.

I saw us on the precipice of our winter years. I do not know how long God will grant either of us but how deeply grateful I am to Him for bringing us together and for allowing us to walk side by side these (at present) thirty-seven years. I do not know of any couple that has a greater marriage than we do. We are often asked the secret to our marriage; while I don't think there is a single secret, there are several things, which are critical. First, live a spirit-filled life; second, be kind… really kind. Third, laugh a lot. Don't take yourself too seriously… look for the humor in life.

Thank you, God, for this precious and godly woman with whom You have allowed me to share my life.

(October 16, 2015)

Photo Credit: Vonda Murdock

A Walk

Autumn chill within the air,
October's days are done
November frost is fading to
December's setting sun.

The path we've walked has been a joy
We faced it with a song
Winter's days are growing short
Our shadows growing long.

Though on our walk it rained sometimes
The sun always broke through
I hardly noticed it at all
For I walked beside of you.

The wind sometimes blew on us, too
But mostly at our back
I raise my hand in praise to Him
Who never let us lack.

The pathway now I see ahead
The road there takes a bend
But hand in hand we'll walk in love
Until our journey end.

The love I feel within my heart
Is deeper than "I do"
I give the glory to my God
Who let me walk with you.

MY LOVE

I love a good love poem. Not the wicked sensual songs that are the rage in the worldly society we live in today, but rather, a man expressing his simple heart-felt love for his wife.

This poem, very clearly, is for my wife, Rachel. She has been the love of my life for nearly forty years and my passion for her is unabated. She is my best friend and closest companion and I crave her fellowship. When I am away from her my heart aches, and I long to rush home.

(November 7, 2015)

My Love

I'll never stop my love for you
In words you say and things you do
Your kindnesses come shining through
I'll never stop my love for you.

The centuries pass, our lives will too
Our memories all will fade from view
I love you, sweet, yes, this is true
I'll never stop my love for you.

From that first day I looked at you
A spring of love within me grew
And permeated through and through
No force could stop my love for you.

When last I part to face my due
To live again in body new
I'll wait for you from Heaven's view
To speak again my love for you.

PROMISES TO KEEP

My favorite poet is Robert Frost, and there are subtle images of his poetry in several of my poems. This poem has direct reference to Frost's poem, "Stopping by the Woods on a Snowy Evening." In that poem, a man would love to pause and rest but is unable to because of promises he must keep. From Garrison Keillor's *The Writer's Almanac*: "Frost wasn't the most successful farmer, but he scrounged up some produce from his farm, hitched up his horse, and took a wagon into town to try and sell enough produce to buy some gifts. He couldn't sell a single thing, and as evening came and it began to snow, he had to head home. He was almost home when he became overwhelmed with the shame of telling his family about his failure, and as if it sensed his mood, the horse stopped, and Frost cried. He recalls he 'bawled like a baby.' Eventually, the horse jingled its bells, and Frost collected himself and headed back home to his family."

My poem is about the duty of a man. In the first two stanzas, he works hard with hope but realizes his life will always be one of toil and labor.

The third stanza is an acceptance of that life of labor as an offering to those he loves. He comes to terms with his role in life and accepts that the reward, clearly not for him but for others, is reasonable. In the last two stanzas, I envisioned that the man turns back into the snow, determined to keep the commitments he made to provide a living to his family. It is a poem about self-sacrifice as an offering of love.

(December 12, 2015)

Promises to Keep

Driving the roads, milestones pass
Destinations untold, yet to see
It matters not, for I've been there before
And it's not where my heart longs to be.

The battles men face, when they labor to race
Too often are not of their choosing
He thinks in the struggle he is winning the fight
But turns to see he is losing.

The prize for his effort in his labor of love
He'll sow but likely won't reap
He longs for his rest but sadly can see
There are miles to go ere he sleeps.

Frost had it right when he stopped by the woods
Pausing to watch falling snow
But promise demanded he press from his pause
Unrested, he knew he must go.

The labor of man is an offering of love
When he has not else he might give
A sacrifice worthy by an unworthy man
He offers that others might live.

A SINGLE RED ROSE

While working in the state of Washington, I traveled from Yakima to Seattle. On the radio, I listened to a Christian talk show for part of the way and heard an interview with an unnamed man (I joined the show late and did not recognize the name) who was asked, "Do you have any big life regrets?" His reply struck my heart. "I think I have not expressed enough to my loved ones that they have my approval."

Approval is an incredible motivator. I know in my own life, the quest for it was responsible for driving me in school and in life to achieve greater successes. But it can also have a destructive side as well. Children might think they can never have their fathers' approval and be driven to unsafe and unwise directions. Their attempts to win approval can be an enduring source of heartache. I pondered this issue for several hours as I continued my drive to the Seattle Airport.

Once in the airport, I rushed to my gate but was stopped by the sight of an elderly man carrying a single red rose. Once on my plane, I considered that rose. The rose is an expression of love, a thing of beauty, and in light of my recent thoughts, a symbol of affirmation. As I flew home to Little Rock, my thoughts turned to my three daughters who were like single red roses to me. I wrote this poem on the plane to honor them.

(February 20, 2016)

A Single Red Rose

The stage light slowly is softened
The curtains lower to close
On the stage someone has lain
A flawless single red rose.

The orchestra ceases their playing
As the conductor steps away
In the hall, thundering silence
There is nothing left to say.

The audience sits in mute silence
As the actor exits to rest
The rose on the stage is so offered
As a "thank you" for doing his best.

When the actor returns to the platform
The audience has left for the night
He's humbled when he spies the red rose
For it means he has done something right.

The rose is the height of all beauty
An expression of love offered all
It reaches to the depths of the spirit
To the heart of another will call.

The rose represents all the beauty
And love given him by his wife
He smiles when he thinks of his daughters
For they are the rose of his life.

III

Poems on Country and the Dream

BEHOLD THE EAGLE

This was the first poem I committed to paper, dated July 4, 1984. In late 1983, I was in the US Air Force on temporary duty to Norway in support of tactical combat operations. During my time there, I broke my leg. After emergent surgery in Norway and additional surgeries back home in South Carolina, I found myself on crutches for nearly a year.

On July 4 the following year (1984), the festivities at Shaw Air Force Base in South Carolina were rather elaborate as we celebrated our nation's independence. One of the Fighter Squadrons had as its symbol the eagle in flight and the fireworks periodically illuminated its massive painting on the side of the building. Braced by crutches, I stood in the crowd that night watching the fireworks and was overcome with pride.

Behold the Eagle

Behold the eagle,
A majestic sight;
The symbol of power,
Of strength in flight.

Dreaming of freedom,
He took to the sky;
When as a young bird
He attempted to fly.

All those around him,
Said, "Give up this dream,
Of flying in clouds,
And of being supreme."

But believing he could,
He stretched out his wing;
And now in the air,
The eagle's the king.

When disbelievers arise,
And your dreams they trample;
Remember the eagle,
And his fine example.

The King of the Air,
This is what he would say,
"We create our tomorrows,
By what we dream today."

THE JOURNEY

I wrote this poem in the desert of Saudi Arabia. I had already been there for several months on temporary duty with the air force.

It is funny how God disrupts our complacency when He desires to steer our lives in a different direction. I found myself, prior to Saudi Arabia, very content and considering a career in the air force even though that was not my dream. But while in Saudi Arabia, I saw the "Peter Principle" in action. The Peter Principle says, in essence, that men continue to get promoted in life until they reach a point where they are unable to perform the job, and there they remain—incompetent in their present position of power. I saw this principle in effect while in Saudi Arabia and I realized this would be a very frustrating career path for me should I remain in the air force (see the back story for my poem "The Best of Men").

I determined that I would explore the possibility of getting out of the air force two years early and begin school. While that plan did not come to fruition, it set me on a path to start taking classes and nearly three years later I was able to separate from the air force and pursue my dream full time.

Many of the poems written in this transitional phase of my life were centered on the pursuit of the dream. It was with very clear direction from the Lord and great encouragement from my wife and family that I was strengthened.

(June 6, 1985)

The Journey

At the height of the mountain,
In the shadow of the tree,
There is born a fearful eagle
A mighty champion he will be.

Countless struggles lie before him,
Many races ahead to run
Many battles that will face him
Ere his pride and rest be won.

His wings are strengthened through failing,
His instincts heightened through loss,
His judgment better through striving,
Although great will be his cost.

His talons ready for battle,
His eyesight sharpened through pain,
Many will try to cage him,
The death of his dream to gain.

Few successes he has counted,
Fewer victories he has known,
But he's still a mighty eagle,
And his dream is still his own.

His desire is yet increasing,
And his goals are aimed so high,
For this eagle is ever striving,
To ensure his dream won't die.

He'll evade each of his captors,
By his desire to be free,
I understand this mighty eagle,
For this eagle, you see, is me.

THE LIGHTHOUSE

This poem was one of a trilogy, taken with the poem "The Journey," written before it, and "The Champion," written after it. This was the critical transitional point in my life where, over a three-month period the decision was made to pursue my dream of going to medical school.

While this poem, like "The Journey" and "The Champion," does not speak of God, please realize, reader, that the decision to leave a safe and secure job was bathed in prayer and in seeking God's will for my life.

Many people say a dreamer is an emotion-led, unstable person. And in many cases, I must agree. I know men, as I'm sure you do as well, who fantasize about one thing after another and jump from job to job, city to city, and even church to church, while their families suffer for their folly. This is foolishness and brings reproach to God. Perhaps when I speak of the "dream," what I really mean is a "vision" for their life—a life's calling. I have heard of pastors and missionaries who have such a dream, or vision, or call of God, which required them to walk away from safety and security in order to follow God. My "dream" was no less a call of God, for I was confident this was His direction for my life and I did not enter into it with disregard for the obstacles. Perhaps this transitional phase of my life was more a process of God reassuring me of His comfort and provision—of me wrestling with the decision to obey Him—and of my surrender to His will.

(August 2, 1985)

Photo Credit: Rachel Veach

The Lighthouse

On the cliff above stood the lighthouse,
Its purpose for this to be:
The light that shone from its windows,
Was there that the traveler might see.

It shone its light in the darkness
In the storms and the blackest of night;
Many owed their lives to its brightness,
So essential was its light.

But the old man who lived there was aging,
And great was his burden to bear;
So I became the apprentice light keeper,
And attempted his labor to share.

On a moonless night I went walking,
'neath the cliff to take a short swim;
but I raced to the lighthouse above me,
when I realized the light had grown dim.

When I got there, the old man was dying,
Taking his last gasp of breath;
These were the words that he whispered
Ere his voice was silenced in death:

"The beacon I've always kept seaward,
On the windows a polish, my son;
Many see, but they won't see it clearly,
That the dream and the beacon are one.

Apathetic and uncaring voices,
Are rising to choke out the light;
But as long as the dream in you liveth,
You've a beacon to shine through the night."

THE CHAMPION

This poem is about perseverance, especially in the face of overwhelming odds. I wrote this poem while driving from Sumter, SC, to Warner Robins, GA, two months after my return from temporary duty in Saudi Arabia.

I had read the first line of the last stanza on a motivational poster (which I typically mock), and I reflected on my dream to go to medical school. There were many "naysayers" in my life at the time—people who did not miss the opportunity to tell me I "didn't have what it took" to go to medical school. Sadly, for a period of time, I believed them. But Rachel, while we walked in the neighborhood around her parent's home late one evening in August 1985, reminded me of her love and undying support. That was enough for me. We had committed our lives to the Lord, and with the firm resolve of my wife to weather any storm in faith, I was encouraged with laser focus to pursue my dream.

(September 2, 1985)

The Champion

The fighter was down, with his blood outward flowing,
'Neath the feet of the victor-to-be;
Through his clouded mind his dream slowly faded,
At the count of the ring referee.

The count stood at three when the fighter awakened,
The crowd had started to chant;
He wanted to win but the struggle seemed hopeless,
And his heart heard his lips say, "I can't."

"I can't" were the words of his heart, truly spoken,
For all faith had fled from his eyes;
Then his dream reappeared, came the victory to focus,
And the fighter attempted to rise.

Although he had given his best to the fight,
Before he was knocked to the floor;
He soon understood when his hope was rekindled,
It was then that he had to give more.

The count had reached six and the fighter was kneeling,
The fire had returned to his eyes;
His courage restored, his spirit then knew,
Self-respect in the dream always lies.

The crowd roared approval, for the fighter now stood,
The count had just reached the nine;
His strength now renewed, he turned to his foe,
Saying, "This time the victory is mine."

The fight then resumed, for the fighter had heart,
Although weary from muscle to bone;
When the smoke and the dust of the battle had cleared,
The fighter was standing alone.

What a dream costs in courage, it gives back in the glory,
For this is the ultimate test;
That the prize would remain to the fighter who fought,
To give his all, and not just his best.

THE GUARDIAN

Another poem in the July 4 series, this poem was inspired by seeing the flag waving at Shaw Air Force Base in South Carolina. I considered that, while it can provide no direct protection to the downtrodden, many had given their life's blood in service to the image of that ideal.

It inspires incredible acts of heroism and bravery and, while often ignored in peace time, when viewed in times of war or national trial will bring even the faint of heart to tears. After all, our flag is not revered for its beauty, design, or its color. It is revered because of the ideal it represents. Freedom. God, please bless America once again with leaders who stand true to its heritage.

(July 4, 1986)

Photo Credit: Vonda Murdock

The Guardian

The guardian stood as a champion would,
In the square of my hometown he stayed;
And the children all played in the grass at his feet,
And a reverence upon him was laid.

As day passed to night, the sentry still stood,
In all weather, save for the rain;
As in battles, now past, where he stood in the grass,
Dying brothers around him had lain.

As days passed to weeks, and weeks into months,
The sentry continued to stand;
The respect of his people reflected in him,
As he viewed his still-free homeland.

He continue to stand, though remembrances came,
Of the battles in which he had fought;
When the odds were against them he rallied his men,
With their blood, the victory was bought.

At the sight of him standing, a pride in his look,
His men then pressed on to the fight;
Their courage renewed when they saw through the smoke,
That he stood at the break of day's light.

But now all is calm in the square of the town,
As the children around him play tag;
Mute witness to battles fought with great pride,
For the guardian is simply... our flag.

THE WINNER'S CIRCLE

Growing up, the historical figure I admired the most was Winston Churchill. His "never quit" philosophy and dogged determination in the face of incredible odds resonated with me even as a boy of twelve.

Medical school was hard. The Lord was faithful throughout as we saw His provision in answers to very specific prayers. It was, however, still a struggle. I tried to continue to hold down a job during the first several years, but this became increasingly difficult. We had Jonathan the week of finals of my first year and Laura the week of finals my third year. Rachel was laid off when Laura was born and we had no income with mounting debts.

Nonetheless, God was so very faithful. We made a conscious decision not to tell *anyone* of our needs and live by faith, convinced that God, who led us on this path, would sustain us in it. And He did. We saw God supplying our very specific needs through the hands of others and our faith grew.

As the medical school senior class president, I would be expected to speak at graduation, only two months away. As Rachel and I sat at a sandwich shop across from the medical school, we wept as we realized *I was going to graduate*. I wrote this poem that night as I recalled the struggles of the past four years and intending to read it as my senior class president's address. But God chose a different path. I was impressed to bestow the honor to a Christian single mother of two children to offer the senior speech. God had honored me by allowing me to graduate!

(March 12, 1994)

The Winner's Circle

Not to the critic does the glory go—
The man who points out every threat
The credit belongs to the man in the fight
Whose face is lined by his sweat.

The man who comes short again and again
And, though failing, will try it once more
On him will the laurels of victory fall
To the one who will rise from the floor.

Not to the timid does the victory come'
To the one who waits in the wings
But the honor is given to the man who is driven
Into the battle his body flings.

Not on the weak will the prize be laid
On the one too afraid to begin
But the one who'll arise again and again
Will achieve through discipline.

Accolades are reserved for the man in the ring
For the one who receives the pain,
Never respect for the frail or the faint
Or the ones who choose to complain.

The statesman of England who cried, "Never quit"
Knew the valley of deep despair
But determined within, saying, "We will win"
And so chose not to languish there.

So I say to you brothers, stand tall once again
Never quit, brush the dust from your face
And the trophy will wait to the congratulate
Each of us... at the winner's place.

VOICES

I have had a number of great encouragers in my life. In addition to my family, two particular men especially stand out: Dr. Ron Grisanti and Bob Johnson.

After my wife, my closest friend is Bob Johnson. He was a constant source of comfort, laughter, and encouragement. When we were struggling in medical school, some members of our church in Columbia, SC, encouraged me to quit so I "could get a job and get caught up" on my bills. Bob was the voice of encouragement who told me not to quit, and for that, I will be forever grateful. He came alongside me, made sure we had what we needed and helped in untold ways. I miss the nights of coffee around one another's table, recalling the working of God in our lives.

The other great encourager in my life was Dr. Ron Grisanti. Sometimes people don't realize the impact "small things" can have on a person's life. I met Ron during medical school at a point of particular struggle. I questioned if I had what it took to complete school and considered quitting. I had, in essence, a crisis of faith. Ron, in a hundred subtle ways, encouraged me to persevere regardless the obstacles.

These men are the voices to me. This poem was written near medical school graduation, as I looked back at the path Rachel and I had walked.

(May 13, 1994)

Voices

In the child's mind are voices,
Saying, "Strive for every dream"
Voices, strong and assuring
Saying, "Things are what they seem."

So the child listens closely
To these voices in his head,
And dreams of what the future holds
as he climbs into his bed.

He dreams of things he could become
Of things he could invent.
Of frontiers he could conquer
In child-like wonderment.

At dawn his eyes are wide-eyed bright
With hope of the day ahead
For he believes he can accomplish
All that his dreams have said.

But as years pass on, the voices fade
For he's told he can never win.
So he faces life with a defeated heart
Dreaming of what might have been.

So year after year his heart heavy grows
As his frame is bent with self-doubt.
In his eye, no flame, but a flicker
Near surrender, he counts himself out.

But into his life God then places a man
Who restores his faith in the dream,
And encourages him to try once again
Not alone, but to work as a team.

So with faith he begins his new journey
Not alone but believing he can.
No longer imprisoned by shadows of fear
For the boy has grown to a man.

In his life, now in flesh, are the voices
Saying, "Don't give up on your dream,
You've hope once again for the future
For NEVER are things as they seem."

THE VETERAN

My eldest daughter Gina and I were driving to an Arkansas Razorback football game. In the course of the drive, she mentioned that she, her sisters, Laura, and Jessica and a friend, Rachel Massey, were in charge of a veteran's program at a local health care facility. They were going to play instruments as an ensemble (piano, viola, violin, cello), read stories, and provide a meal for the veterans. She mentioned that she would like to read a new poem to them and could I write one?

Of course, the rest of the drive we dedicated to writing this poem (I dictated as she scribed). By the time we arrived for the game, the poem was finished. As an eleven-year air force veteran myself, I think it captures the deep respect and honor these men and women deserve. May God bless you, veterans.

(November 27, 2015)

Photo Credit: Public Domain

The Veteran

With furrowed brow he sat alone
Memories a shadow cast
Brothers he had fought beside
Now in distant past.

He swore an oath to honor
Flag, country, liberty
His sacrifice and acts of faith
Served to make men free.

But what of him, this selfless man
Who gave us all he had
In answer to his country's call
Left mother, wife, and dad?

He charged into the face of war
Obeying orders given
Knowing death might meet him there
He was by honor driven.

Can any count the worth of him?
Mere words his story tell?
Who faithful stood within the gap
While brothers round him fell?

God bless you, men, for what you've done
In service to liberty
We stand before you with humble salute
In gratitude honor thee.

WARRIOR

Only two weeks after writing "The Veteran," I wrote this poem. I don't write many free verse poems but this one, I felt, was the only way to convey the message I wanted to share. In the emergency room this night, I was treating an elderly woman with a serious medical problem. Her husband, a silent man in an old tattered coat, and her daughter, who was the family spokesperson, accompanied her.

After several long discussions on her mothers condition and test results, the daughter pulled me aside and apologized for her father, who had sat in the room silent during the entire visit. "He doesn't speak much but he watches everything like a hawk." She went on to say that he had won numerous combat medals for bravery in wartime, yet was a soft-spoken humble man at home.

That evening as I pondered our conversation, I realized that this, great, brave man who had lived a selfless life was a warrior in the truest sense of the word, yet now was cloaked as an old man, tattered by life, and to the eyes of many, useless. May God open our eyes to see the unlovely, the throw-aways, those worthy of honor yet cast aside by a blind world. These are the Warriors cloaked.

(December 12, 2015)

Photo Credit: Rachel Veach

Warrior

am i nothing to you as you pass me by?

> Alone I charged a squad of enemy soldiers with nothing but a rifle and anger.

do you see me?

> I sang and danced and fell in love as a young man.

can you see me?

> The sacrifice I gave on that field of battle left me broken but I would do it again even now.

look past what you see, to see me

> When I charged certain death, duty and honor were not just words.

DO YOU SEE ME?

> ... or do you see an old man in a tattered coat sitting alone on a bench?

> I am a warrior... cloaked.

IV

Tributes

TODAY

I am convinced that being an emergency room physician is not for the faint of heart. I had a colleague who described the work as "hours of boredom punctuated by moments of sheer terror." I think that is an accurate description; one moment you are treating countless colds, ear infections, and sore throats and within seconds are dealing with a gunshot wound to the chest. I absolutely love the work!

There are times however, where I wish there was a "reset" button… or a place to escape to. This particular day in Russellville, AR, I was treating "run of the mill" cases in the ER. An elderly couple walked in with the wife complaining of chest pain. With those words, "chest pain," a different gear clicks in ER physicians and nurses and the next fifteen minutes were a flurry of activity, IVs, medications, and diagnostic tests.

I allowed the eighty-year-old man to stay in the room with his wife while we worked feverishly with her. "I'm sorry," she kept repeating over and over, embarrassed for the attention. He just kept patting her hand and once kissed her forehead. Despite our efforts, her aged heart was not strong enough to survive the massive heart attack she was experiencing and she took her last breath this side of eternity.

This poem was written from a broken heart as I grieved with him his wife's death.

(September 19, 1997)

242

Today

Today I sat with a man
And told him I did all I could do...
But it just wasn't enough.

Today I sat with a man
And heard him tell of the fifty years
He had spent with his wife.

He stopped mid sentence and looked up at me,
... eyes lined with the
wrinkles of experience.

"I loved her," he said as I sat and listened.

Today I sat with a man
And heard the deep sadness in his voice
"She was a good woman..." his voice trailed
off into nothingness

"What will I do, now?"

Today I sat with a man
... and learned the lesson of silence.

A TRIBUTE

On February 12, 2012, Dr. Don Jasmin was our guest speaker at our church's second anniversary. It was also his sixtieth anniversary in the ministry. Researching a little about his ministry and work over the last few years and his fondness of using the phrase "No compromise," I wrote this poem. Our pastor had it engraved on a plaque for him as we honored him for his service to the Lord over sixty years.

(February 12, 2012)

A Tribute

Over sixty years, an arrow true
And to the Savior many drew
Through trials, tested, not a few
Firm resolve, the Savior knew.

The strength to live for God arise
To serve our Lord, the certain prize
This edict then we must surmise
That by God's grace, no compromise.

BIRTH OF A MINISTRY

My pastor, Dr. Terry L. Coomer, has founded several counseling ministries, each out of personal hardship. The first ministry, "For the Love of the Family," started more than thirty years ago because he saw a great need for ministering to families in the raising of children. The second counseling ministry, "Hope Biblical Counseling," started in 2015 as he saw a great need to counsel pastors, assistant pastors, and missionaries to walk in the Spirit.

This poem was written in celebration of the founding of his "For the Love of the Family" ministry. This ministry was born out of deep heartache. His wife was near death during childbirth and he had been told that neither she nor his unborn daughter would survive. In prayer throughout the night, he was assured by God in the morning that they would survive. The commitment he made to God during that night was the foundation for the "For the Love of the Family" ministry.

Through this ministry, we have seen countless marriages restored and children rescued and given opportunities to live lives useful to the Savior.

(May 20, 2012)

Birth of a Ministry

Broken, at a time of despair and grief
Loved ones in the balance hang,
A man in the night on bended knee
Through prayer, Heaven's bells then rang.

Victory, not seen, but promised sure,
"Lord, will you spare their life?
Yearning as I am to follow Your way,
Will You restore my daughter and wife?"

"Dust I am, yet loved by God,
Submitted to the Rock more than I".
All through the night he sought His face,
Uncertain as to His reply.

"Son, their lives I'll restore to you,"
The Lord's answer came at the morn,
"But you must commit, their way wisely guide,"
And "For the Love of the Family" was born.

POEM SCRIPTURE REFERENCE

Ruth	Kinsman Redeemer
1 Sam 2:3	My Praise
Neh. 12	Sacrifice of Praise
Ps. 19:12	My Praise
Ps. 23	My Shepherd
Ps. 32:8	This My Plea
Ps. 33	Psalm 33
Ps. 51	Servant Leadership
Ps. 84	Your House
Ps. 85:10	Inscribed Nails
Ps. 90	Time Spent in Psalm 90
Ps. 90:8	My Praise
Ps. 119:4–16	Rise Above
Prov. 5:22	The Unstable Man
Prov. 13:1	The Scorner
Prov. 13:14	The Light
Prov. 14:6	The Scorner
Prov. 16:25	What it is and What it's Not; The Way of Man
Is. 6:6	Hear Am I
Is. 11:2	Hear Am I
Is. 32:17, 18	Blessed Reassurance
Is. 53:10–11	Unworthy
Jer. 17:10	My Praise
Jer. 18:1–6	The Potter's Field
Jer. 31	My Shepherd
Jer. 33:11	Sacrifice of Praise
Lam. 3:23	This My Plea
Hos. 4–7	Come Ye Out

ABOUT THE AUTHOR

Dr. Paul Veach is a board certified emergency medicine physician who still practices medicine in the Little Rock, Arkansas, area. He is a well-respected professional and is a much sought speaker in the field of emergency medicine across the nation. As an ER medical director and supervisor of more than twenty ERs, he has seen the best and worst that society has to offer…and recognizes that the world's greatest need is Jesus Christ.

Through his daily reading, reflection, and meditation in the Word of God, he has developed a unique perspective in the application of scripture to our daily walk. God has gifted him with the ability to find, in even difficult passages of scripture, the poetry God provided so it makes a connection to the heart of the reader.

Married for nearly forty years to his sweetheart, Rachel, they have raised five children. As a Sunday school teacher for the "Pastor's Class" and music minister for more than twenty years, his poetry sometimes reflects difficult themes ("Visions of Zechariah") as well as comic turns ("A Story Bears Telling"). He and his wife have conducted numerous marriage seminars and have recorded four sacred music CDs.